Facilitating LGBTQIA+ Allyship through Multimodal Writing in the Elementary Classroom

T0372851

This book reports findings of a qualitative study intended to disrupt notions of heteronormativity among preservice elementary teachers by engaging them in multimodal writing and text production around issues facing LGBTQIA+ youth.

Against the backdrop of increasing anti-transgender sentiment in the United States, the text highlights the necessity of integrating queered pedagogy in teacher education to facilitate candidates' movement through the continuum and leave them prepared, equipped, and willing to support children identifying as LGBTQIA+. Through analysis of picture books, infographics, and multimodal texts produced by teacher candidates, this cutting-edge volume develops a continuum of engagement, from apathy through to active allyship, with LGBTQIA+ youth.

This timely volume will benefit researchers, academics, and educators with an interest in gender and sexuality studies, primary and elementary education, as well as teacher education more specifically. Those involved with queer theory and the sociology of education will also benefit from this volume.

Judith M. Dunkerly, PhD, is an associate professor of literacy, language & culture in the Department of Teaching and Learning at the Darden College of Education and Professional Studies, Old Dominion University, USA.

Julia Poplin, PhD, is an assistant professor of social foundations of education in the College of Education and Social Services at Minnesota State University, Moorhead, USA.

Valerie Sledd Taylor, PhD, is the director of the office of clinical experiences in the Darden College of Education and Profession Studies at Old Dominion University, USA.

Routledge Critical Studies in Gender and Sexuality in Education

Series Editors: Wayne Martino, EJ Renold, Goli Rezai-Rashti, Jessica Ringrose and Nelson Rodriguez

7 **Lad Culture in Higher Education**
Sexism, Sexual Harassment and Violence
Carolyn Jackson and Vanita Sundaram

8 **Queer, Trans, and Intersectional Theory in Educational Practice**
Student, Teacher, and Community Experiences
Cris Mayo and Mollie V. Blackburn

9 **Young British African and Caribbean Men Achieving Educational Success**
Disrupting Deficit Discourses about Black Male Achievement
Cecile Wright, Uvanney Maylor, and Thomas Pickup

10 **The Experiences of Queer Students of Color at Historically White Institutions**
Navigating Intersectional Identities on Campus
Antonio Duran

11 **Affect and the Making of the Schoolgirl**
A New Materialist Perspective on Gender Inequity in Schools
Melissa Joy Wolfe

12 **Facilitating LGBTQIA+ Allyship through Multimodal Writing in the Elementary Classroom**
Preparing Teachers to Challenge Heteronormativity
Judith M. Dunkerly, Julia Poplin, and Valerie Sledd Taylor

For more information about this series, please visit: https://www.routledge.com/Routledge-Critical-Studies-in-Gender-and-Sexuality-in-Education/book-series/RCSGSE

Facilitating LGBTQIA+ Allyship through Multimodal Writing in the Elementary Classroom

Preparing Teachers to Challenge Heteronormativity

Judith M. Dunkerly, Julia Poplin, and Valerie Sledd Taylor

Routledge
Taylor & Francis Group
NEW YORK AND LONDON

First published 2022
by Routledge
605 Third Avenue, New York, NY 10158

and by Routledge
4 Park Square, Milton Park, Abingdon, Oxon, OX14 4RN

Routledge is an imprint of the Taylor & Francis Group, an informa business

Library of Congress Cataloging-in-Publication Data
A catalog record for this book has been requested

ISBN: 978-0-367-62818-5 (hbk)
ISBN: 978-0-367-62819-2 (pbk)
ISBN: 978-1-003-11093-4 (ebk)

DOI: 10.4324/9781003110934

Typeset in Times New Roman
by Apex CoVantage, LLC

I would like to dedicate this book to three remarkable young men and to my mother. To my children, Cam and Shannon, you are my "why" in everything I do. Thank you for your insights and inspiration. To my nephew Raymond M. Cruz, you left us far too early, but your light shines brighter still. ***#RayStrong****. For my mom, Gayle Adair Garrett, who passed away from COVID-19 as we were finishing this book, may the fierce love you modeled be reflected in this work as well.*

J.M.D.

The authors Julia and Valerie would like to dedicate this work and all its efforts to Cam, who has taught us that "we know exactly what to do . . . but, in a much more real sense, we have no idea what to do" (Michael Scott, Season 5 – Episode 13). Thank you for teaching us so much we did not, and could not, know without you. The privilege to be your ally, advocate, and family is the greatest.

Contents

Figures and Tables

Figures

Tables

Acknowledgments

Land Acknowledgment

Minnesota:

> Minnesota State University Moorhead acknowledges that it occupies the ancestral land of the Anishinaabe (Ojibwe), Dakota (Sisseton, Wahpeton), and Yanktonai Dakota First Nations.
> We strive to build toward a better relationship between our university and the indigenous people still present with us.

Virginia:

> We acknowledge that we are on the traditional territory of the Powhatan Confederacy, Tsenacommacah, Chesapeake, and Nansemond peoples. To recognize the land is an expression of gratitude and appreciation to those whose territory you reside on and a way of honoring the Indigenous people who have been living and working on the land from time immemorial. It is important to understand the long-standing history that has brought you to reside on the land and to seek to understand your place within that history. Land acknowledgments do not exist in past tense or historical context: colonialism is a current ongoing process, and we need to build mindfulness of our present participation.

Slavery Acknowledgment

We cannot separate the history of our community from the history of colonialism and slavery in the United States. Four hundred years ago, the first enslaved Africans were brought to Point Comfort – just 16 miles from our university. We acknowledge the legacy of slavery in this area and the blood, sweat, and tears of enslaved people that soak the earth in Hampton Roads, Virginia. This legacy persists today, as we continue to work toward racial equity, liberation, and community.

From the Authors

This monograph is the culminating act of a year-long study. Yet, more importantly, it is also a call to action and a reminder that every one of us has the privilege and responsibility to be an ally. We are grateful to the students of our courses for their honesty, their vulnerability, and most importantly, as future elementary teachers, their willingness to grow in their allyship along with us. We also thank Dr. Helen Crompton and Cathleen Rhodes for their invaluable participation and contributions to this study.

We acknowledge as well the funding that made this study possible. Our thanks as well to Remica Bingham-Risher, the Director of Quality Enhancement Plan Initiatives, for supporting our research and for your boundless enthusiasm. We would also like to thank the Safe Space Team at Old Dominion University and the LGBT Life Center in Norfolk, VA, for visiting our classes and being so generous in your time and expertise. Our deepest gratitude as well to LGBTQIA+ researchers, activists, and allies from whom we have learned so much and who inspire us to work toward justice and equity for the LGBTQIA+ community, especially its youngest members. Finally, our heartfelt thanks to our editorial team at Routledge, especially Elsbeth Wright and AnnaMary Goodall for their encouragement, patience, and expertise, without which this book would not have been possible.

1 Introduction

As we prepare this book for publication, we do so against a wave of anti-transgender legislation sweeping the United States. Thirty-three states have introduced more than 100 bills, some already passed into law, that are a severe threat to the life, liberty, and pursuit of happiness of transgender individuals and that cruelly targets transgender youth. This is occurring across the backdrop of historic increases in anti-trans violence in the United States. As David Alphonse, the President of the Human rights Campaign, poignantly stated:

> This year, we reached two grim milestones – [we] recorded the most deaths of transgender and gender non-conforming people of any year since we began tracking this violence, and we have documented more than 200 total deaths. . . . Divisive and dehumanizing rhetoric from anti-equality political leaders has contributed to the toxic mix of racism, sexism, and transphobia that drives this horrific violence.
>
> (Roberts, 2020)

This combination of increased violence and legislative discrimination marks this a truly perilous time for LGBTQIA+ youth, especially those who identify as transgender. At this writing, the state of Arkansas became the first to outlaw providing gender-affirming treatment to minors (Krishnakumar, 2021). According to the LGBTQIA+ advocacy organization, Human Rights Campaign, this is the highest number of bills in a current legislative session since they began tracking data in 2015. The bills target everything from so-called "bathroom bills" which have been largely challenged, to more specifically aimed at transgender youth, specifically in banning transgender teens from participating in same-gender youth sports, and perhaps even more insidiously, making it a crime for medical professionals to provide gender-affirming care to minors (Human Rights Campaign, 2021). According to demographic statistics based on where transgender adolescents reside in the United States, these bills could impact one in four transgender individuals (Herman et al., 2017).

DOI: 10.4324/9781003110934-1

Most of these bills are framed around conservative notions of "protecting" children from potentially invasive procedures, for example, HB 1570 is named "The Arkansas Save Adolescents from Experimentation Act (SAFE)." Although there is no scientific evidence or major medical opinions that support the notion that providing gender-affirming care to minors is at all harmful, 20 states introduced legislation in this session that would prevent minors from receiving gender-affirming treatment. Alabama introduced a bill to make it a felony for medical professionals to provide transition-related care to transgender minors, while Arkansas passed its legislation despite a veto from the governor. The most recent manifestations of discrimination – banning sports participation and denying appropriate medical care – single out for discrimination a population already at higher risk for suicide, self-harm, and depression (Thoma et al., 2019).

Drawing from my (Judith's) own personal experiences with my son, Cam, I can speak to the impact of discrimination on a child based only on ignorance and/or fear. When Cam was 15, he came out (at least to close family) as transgender. At the time, he was attending a small, private school due to bullying he was facing in a public school. While I was very hesitant for him to remain in a nonsecular environment that forced a duplicitous existence (the school taught that any relationship or identity beyond the binary was sinful and cause for expulsion), Cam wanted to remain as his best friend was in her final year at the school. At the same time, Cam had started hormone therapy which was deepening his voice and causing a more masculine appearance. The situation came to an unfortunate conclusion when the school expelled Cam for reporting that his social studies teacher intimated that gay individuals "deserved" to be killed in the Holocaust and did not intervene when his classmates advocated for the execution and/or sterilization of transgender individuals. These events led Cam to experience severe depression and anxiety that led to self-injurious behaviors. While he is now a thriving senior who enjoys the full support and advocacy of his public high school, the scars, literal and figurative, remain. Although Cam's experiences at school were in a sense extreme, we are beginning to see a glimmer of societal hope regarding increasing allyship and support for young people identifying as LGBTQIA+.

For example, the 2020 American Library Association (ALA) "Rainbow Book List" examined over 550 children's books with LGBTQIA+ characters or themes to select the 92 titles for the list, citing an

> abundance of genre fiction, as well as books whose plots do not revolve around anxiety concerning a queer character's identity. We've also seen an increase in books with non-binary, asexual-spectrum, and bisexual characters.
>
> (Breitenbach, 2020)

As other scholars have pointed out, representation, inclusion, and the decolonization of educational spaces matter in race, culture, family structure, and most assuredly in gender expression and sexual orientation (Edelsky, 1994; Ladson-Billings, 2006; Möller, 2020; Thomas, 2016).

We are heartened by the increase in LGBTQIA+ children's and young adult literature available and making its way into classrooms (Blackburn, Clark, & Nemeth, 2015; Blackburn & Clark, 2011). Similarly, the existence of Gay/Straight Alliances in high schools and some middle schools has also been increasing (GLSEN, 2016). However, little has been enacted in teacher education programs – especially at the primary/elementary level. We believe that providing preservice elementary teacher candidates with the knowledge and dispositions to address issues facing LGBTQIA+ youth is imperative and represents a significant gap in the current literature.

We contend that elementary educators have always been on the front lines of societal change, yet often face substantial resistance and backlash from other stakeholders which often limits their efforts. For example, Cumming-Potvin and Martino (2014) found that although elementary teachers they interviewed after reading LGBTQIA+-inclusive literature expressed a desire to teach inclusively, their actual practice involved avoiding or reframing the content of LGBTQIA+ children's literature ran counter to their stated desire for inclusivity. For example, the teachers ignored the characters' sexual orientation and/or attempted to disingenuously portray the characters as single parents. The researchers reported, "a recurrent theme [of] fear, mindfulness, or cautiousness concerning the surveillance of the parental community" (p. 314). Indeed, this fear and cautiousness may become more pronounced when teachers "begin to recognize their role in the historical silence surrounding LGBTQ identities . . . [and start] to take stock of cultural norms that maintain cis-heteronormativity in their unique school contexts" (Staley & Leonardi, 2019, p. 30). For the purposes of this study, we define cis-heteronormativity as the "societal assumptions and norms which are based on heterosexual, cisgender experiences influenced by social biases, privileges, and stereotyping" (Carrotte et al., 2016; p. 1). However, this extends past cisgender/heterosexual privilege. These cisgender, heterosexual assumptions and the seemingly unshakeable myth of binary gender identities permeate and influence societal values and policies to the pointed detriment and oppression of those identifying beyond fixed binary states.

These recursive elements of fear, parental/community surveillance, and the dawning realization of the oppression of LGBTQIA+ identities fueled by cisnormativity were very apparent in this study and certainly posed a stumbling block as our students navigated their own beliefs, attitudes, and the realities faced by LGBTQIA+ children and families in the public school system.

Overview of Chapters

Chapter 2. Invisible Rainbow: LGBTQIA+ Representation in Elementary Schools and Elementary Teacher Education Programs

In this chapter, we illustrate for the reader the statistics and challenges faced by LGBTQIA+ children and their parents in elementary schools and the lack of purposeful and sustained LGBTQIA+ inclusion in teacher preparation programs in the United States. We recognize children identifying as LGBTQIA+ do so as young as kindergarten (McEntarfer, 2016). However, teacher education programs are woefully underprepared to address the particular needs of LGBTQIA+ children as part of their curriculum. In addition, the dominance of heteronormative positions can be traced to the global issue of homophobic and transphobic bullying in violation of human rights (UNESCO, 2012). While middle schools and high schools often have Gay/Straight Alliances and more visible resources for students, they are less frequently available in the primary/elementary grades. Moreover, elementary teachers are often more reluctant than their middle and high school counterparts to address the identities of, and issues faced by, LGBTQIA+ children out of fear of parental or administrative pushback over the "appropriateness" of the topic, materials used, or whether it belongs in the classroom at all. Meyer, Quantz, Taylor & Peter (2019) found that elementary educators were also less likely to report participating in LGBTQ-inclusive efforts at their schools than secondary educators (22% versus 47%) and 20% of all participants reported that their "students are too young" to discuss LGBTQ topics in their curriculum. As a perhaps not surprising result, children identifying as LGBTQIA+ in elementary schools experience being stigmatized and face a greater risk of bullying, depression, and self-harm.

This is unfortunately unsurprising given the dearth of representation of these issues in teacher preparation education. In our program, well over 65% of candidates felt that they were either "under-prepared or not at all prepared" for LGBTQIA+ students in their classroom, a percentage that largely reflects other teacher education programs. This was especially true of the candidates being confident or comfortable in welcoming children who identify as transgender. Organizations such as GLSEN (2016) among others report that transgender children and youth are especially a risk in schools. Recent data indicate that 75% of the more than 150,000 transgender students in middle school and high school in the United States felt unsafe because of their gender expression. As the mother (Judith) of a transgender teen, I see my child in those statistics (Dunkerly-Bean & Ross, 2018). As a teacher educator, it is very clear that more needs to be done to address this in teacher preparation programs. Indeed, Martino (2013) calls for:

> [N]ot only a special focus on transgender and nonconforming identities in teacher education curricula but also a systematic effort and critical commitment to addressing the very privileging of the hegemonic systems that constrain and curtail a more just politics of gender expression and embodiment within the context of teacher education.
>
> (p. 171)

Thus, we address the lack of inclusionary and anti-oppressive instruction in elementary teacher education programs, and how those manifest in the colonizing effects of heteronormativity, especially as it relates to cisgender assumptions of teacher candidates.

Chapter 3. Multimodal Literacies and LGBTQIA+ Children's Literature: Writing the Rainbow

Chapter 3 provides an overview of multimodal literacies, digital texts, and the use of LGBTQIA+ inclusive children's literature to facilitate social justice. Drawing from exemplar studies, we examine how past research has leveraged the affordances of digital activism to raise awareness of systemic inequities. From the digital texts and multimodal literacies evident in the *#MeToo, Black Lives Matter* (Price-Dennis & Carrion, 2017), *#IRunwithAhmed*, to name a few, digital communication changes the ways we present, re-present, and share knowledge individually and internationally (Price-Dennis & Carrion, 2017). In this chapter then, we offer some exemplars from previous research that has drawn from multimodal or digital writing to expand the possibilities for teacher education with and from a social justice lens. We also provide an overview of previous research that has used children's and/or Young Adult (YA) literature to provide mirrors, windows, and sliding glass doors (O'Byrne, 2019; McNair & Edwards, 2021) to facilitate acceptance of and advocacy for LGBTQIA+ people.

Given the omnipresent use of digital and multimodal literacies in our students' lives, we drew from culturally responsive teaching practices (Ladson-Billings, 2006) to engage our students across courses and assignments pertinent to this project. We also briefly review how previous research has sought to incorporate LGBTQIA+ children's and/or young adult literature in teacher preparation, as well as some of the challenges and resistance faced by teacher educators when including this in their courses. The chapter concludes with a description of how we selected

LGBTQIA+ inclusive text sets and facilitated workshops to explore various forms of multimodal literacy including digital book creation with our students.

Chapter 4. Challenging Teacher Candidate's Heteronormative Assumptions: Our Theoretical Approach and Methodology

In Chapter 4, we outline the theoretical framework of queered pedagogy (Jagose, 1996; Miller, 2015; Simon et al., 2019; Blackburn & Clark, 2011) and the analytical frameworks we designed to explain the range of reactions and texts produced by the teacher candidates. While the original intent of the study was to produce a digital repository of exemplary texts for classroom use, we found that, instead, what we were witnessing was a continuum of attitudes and artifacts that we denoted as "Dimensions of Allyship." We created this framework in part by drawing from a model that describes three dimensions of citizenship (Westheimer, 2015; Westheimer & Kahne, 2004).

Utilizing a qualitative case study approach (Stake, 1995), we designed activities and arranged for members of the local LGBTQIA+ community to come in and work with our students in two different courses (Instructional Technology & PK-6 English Language Arts Methods) over two semesters (fall 2018 and spring 2019). While the contexts and content of each of these courses were different, we utilized an overarching theoretical framework of queer pedagogy to encourage students to read, and in our case, write, through the perspective of queer theory (Jagose, 1996; Miller, 2015; Simon et al., 2019; Blackburn & Clark, 2011). Heather McEntarfer (2016), posits, "queer pedagogy also asks both students and teachers to look inward. It asks us all to be open to a "reflexive and tentative journey into the unknown and unexamined 'differences and oppressors within" (p. 300). This was certainly true in this study and served to inform our approach as both teachers and researchers.

Chapter 5. The Dimensions of Allyship Framework: Stages and Progressions

In this chapter, we describe the Dimensions of Allyship framework and the four stages that comprise it. In providing examples of the candidate's artifacts and interview comments, we seek here to illustrate how we engaged in an open dialogic exchange (Bakhtin, 1981) to push back at their resistance rather than criticizing or demonizing their responses. In the case of disengaged candidates, we found that their artifacts and comments centered on themes of isolationism, "othering" ("they" choose this lifestyle . . .), and profound fear of negative consequences from various stakeholders for engaging with the topic. As is certainly evidenced in these challenging times, strict adherence to opposing views or attempting to silence the Other is counterproductive. Rather, we saw this as an opportunity to acknowledge their position and yet, also draw parallels between civil and human rights that cannot be subject to individual viewpoints or religious beliefs. We were also able to discuss recent scholarship calling for religious schools to recognize that the discrimination directed at LGBTQIA+ youth is antithetical to Christian ethics of justice (Joldersma, 2016). Moreover, for students who were tempted to ridicule or chastise those who were disengaged, there was an opportunity to discuss anti-religious views as a bias within itself (Mcentarfer, 2016).

In contrast, the students who reflected passive engagement tended to circumnavigate the issues faced by the LGBTQIA+ community by comparing them to those who are discriminated against because of race or culture but in a manner analogous to a "colorblind" approach. This too provided an opportunity for dialogue, but in many ways, these students held more steadfastly to their viewpoints and were less easily moved than the apathetic or disengaged. Much like how whiteness operates as frequently covert oppression, we saw that this position held a cisgender perspective as normative. Many of these candidates simply believed that being a member of the LGBTQIA community was not unlike being a member of a historically nondominant race or culture. Their artifacts and comments centered on tolerance and acceptance; however, it was as measured against a straight, cisgender identity. Of all the stages in our framework, this group is perhaps the most challenging as their positioning may be the most resistant to allyship as they believed tolerance alone was the goal.

The remaining two stages of our framework – empathetic responsiveness and allyship – represent an authentic advocacy stance by our candidates. While these two stages somewhat resemble each other, there are some notable differences. Namely, teacher candidates exhibiting empathetic responsiveness focused on combatting stereotypes (i.e., same-sex parents, traditional gender roles). Additionally, their artifacts attempted to normalize a variety of gender expressions of identity (i.e., pronoun use, nonbinary appearances). For the sake of operationalizing the definition of allyship, we draw from GLSEN who espouses that allies recognize intersectionality, use their cisgender privilege to combat oppression, recognize Black & Brown queerness rather than only LGBT White individuals, and finally promote greater acknowledgment of trans people.

By contrast, those candidates whose comments and artifacts reflected allyship advocated for straight and/or cisgender people to actively engage in anti-discriminatory practices and to stand with the community. The books and conversations that were identified as fitting in this category exemplified teachers as advocates in close alignment with the GLSEN definition as well as descriptions of what it means to be an ally to other marginalized groups (Love, 2019).

Chapter 6. Challenges and Affordances: Preparing Elementary Teacher Candidates to Be Allies

Our final chapter discusses the challenges and affordances in creating spaces in teacher education programs for not only awareness of LGBTQIA+ awareness but also allyship. While having candidates engage in discussions with LGBTQIA+ community members, conduct research, and create multimodal texts is only one point of entry, we believe it to be a meaningful one. In addition, our data reflected that candidates felt more prepared to welcome LGBTQIA+ children and families into their future classrooms and believed themselves to be more knowledgeable and empathetic than they were at the start. However, as we have illustrated in previous chapters, this was not the case for all students and indicates the need for the inclusion of LGBTQIA+ topics in the elementary teacher preparation. While individual teacher candidates themselves may well be anti-homophobic/transphobic, they are not given the tools, experiences, or resources to extend their personal beliefs into their professional identities and practice. We conclude with a call for much-needed allyship in teacher education programs and provide implications and suggestions for the furtherance of this work.

References

Bakhtin, M. M. (1981). *The dialogic imagination: Four essays by M. M. Bakhtin* (M. Holquist, Ed.; C. Emerson & M. Holquist, Trans.). Austin: University of Texas Press.

Blackburn, M. V., & Clark, C. T. (2011). Analyzing talk in a long-term literature discussion group: Ways of operating within LGBT-inclusive and queer discourses. *Reading Research Quarterly*, *46*(3), 222–248.

Blackburn, M. V., Clark, C. T., & Nemeth, E. A. (2015). Examining queer elements and ideologies in LGBT-themed literature: What queer literature can offer young adult readers. *Journal of Literacy Research*, *47*(1), 11–48.

Breitenbach, K. (2020, February 5). The 2020 Rainbow Book List. https://glbtrt.ala.org/rainbowbooks/archives/1331

Carrotte, E. R., Vella, A. M., Bowring, A. L., Douglass, C., Hellard, M. E., & Lim, M. S. (2016). "I am yet to encounter any survey that actually reflects my life": A qualitative study of inclusivity in sexual health research. *BMC Medical Research Methodology*, *16*(1), 1–10.

Cumming-Potvin, W., & Martino, W. (2014). Teaching about queer families: Surveillance, censorship, and the schooling of sexualities. *Teaching Education*, *25*(3), 309–333.

Dunkerly-Bean, J., & Ross, C. (2018). Not the girl everyone sees: A transgender teen's experiences in a faith-based school. *English Journal, 108*(2), 95–97.

Edelsky, C. (1994). Education for democracy. *Language Arts, 71*(4), 252–257.

GLSEN. (2016). *The 2015 national school climate survey: The experiences of lesbian, gay, bisexual, transgender, and queer youth in our nation's schools.* Retrieved from www.glsen.org/article/2015-national-school-climate-survey

Herman, J. L., Flores, A. R., Brown, T. N. T., Wilson, B. D. M., & Conron, K. J. (2017). *Age of individuals who identify as transgender in the United States*. Los Angeles, CA: The Williams Institute.

Human Rights Campaign Foundation. (2021). LGBTQ Definitions for Children. Welcoming Schools. https://welcomingschools.org/resources/definitions-lgbtq-elementary-school.

Jagose, A. (1996). *Queer theory: An introduction*. New York: New York University Press.

Joldersma, C. W. (2016). Doing justice today: A welcoming embrace for LGBT students in Christian schools. *International Journal of Christianity & Education, 20*(1), 32–48.

Krishnakumar, P. (2021). This record-breaking year for anti-transgender legislation would affect minors the most. *CNN*. Retrieved from www.cnn.com/2021/04/15/politics/antitransgender-legislation-2021/index. html

Ladson-Billings, G. (2006). Yes, but how do we do it? Practicing culturally relevant pedagogy. In J. Landsman & C. W. Lewis (Eds.), *White teachers/ diverse classrooms: A guide to building inclusive schools, promoting high expectations, and eliminating racism* (pp. 29–42). Sterling, VA: Stylus.

Love, B. (2019). *We want to do more than survive: Abolitionist teaching and the pursuit of educational freedom*. Boston, MA: Beacon Press.

Martino, W. (2013). An invaluable resource for supporting transgender, transsexual, and gender non-conforming students in school communities: A review of supporting transgender and transsexual students in K-12 schools. *Journal of LGBT Youth, 10*(1–2), 169–172.

McEntarfer, H. K. (2016). *Navigating gender and sexuality in the classroom: Narrative insights from students and educators*. New York: Routledge.

McNair, J. C., & Edwards, P. A. (2021). The Lasting Legacy of Rudine Sims Bishop: Mirrors, Windows, Sliding Glass Doors, and More. *Literacy Research: Theory, Method, and Practice, 70*(1), 202–212.

Meyer, E. J., Quantz, M., Taylor, C., & Peter, T. (2019). Elementary teachers' experiences with LGBTQ-inclusive education: Addressing fears with knowledge to improve confidence and practices. *Theory Into Practice, 58*(1), 6–17.

Miller, S. J. (2015). A queer literacy framework promoting (a) gender and (a) sexuality self-determination and justice. *English Journal*, 37–44.

Möller, K. J. (2020). Reading and responding to LGBTQ-inclusive children's literature in school settings: Considering the state of research on inclusion. *Language Arts, 97*(4), 235–251.

O'Byrne, W. I. (2019). Educate, empower, advocate: Amplifying marginalized voices in a digital society. *Contemporary Issues in Technology and Teacher Education, 19*(4), 640–669.

Price-Dennis, D., & Carrion, S. (2017). Leveraging digital literacies for equity and social justice. *Language Arts, 94*(3), 190.

Roberts, M. (2020). Marking the Deadliest Year on Record, HRC Releases Report on Violence Against Transgender and Gender Non-Conforming People. *Human Rights Campaign.*

Simon, R., Walkland, T., Gallagher, B., Evis, S., & Baer, P. (2018). Breaking gender expectations: Adolescents' critical rewriting of a trans young adult novel. In *Literacies, sexualities, and gender* (pp. 141–154). New York: Routledge.

Stake, R. W. (1995). *The art of case study research.* Thousand Oaks, CA: Sage.

Thoma, B. C., Salk, R. H., Choukas-Bradley, S., Goldstein, T. R., Levine, M. D., & Marshal, M. P. (2019). Suicidality disparities between transgender and cisgender adolescents. *Pediatrics, 144*(5).

Thomas, E. E. (2016). Stories still matter: Rethinking the role of diverse children's literature today. *Language Arts, 94*(2), 11.

UNESCO. (2012). *Education sector response to homophobic bullying.* Paris, France: Author.

Westheimer, J. (2015). *What kind of citizen: Educating our children for the common good.* New York: Teachers College Press.

Westheimer, J., & Kahne, J. (2004). What kind of citizen? The politics of educating for democracy. *American Educational Research Journal, 41*(2), 237–269.

2 Invisible Rainbow

LGBTQIA+ Representation in Elementary Schools and Elementary Teacher Education Programs

This chapter discusses the often-negative experiences of LGBTQIA+ children and their families in schools, and the lack of representation of LGBTQIA+ inclusion in the curriculum of teacher education preparation that undoubtedly contributed to them. Despite alarming statistics regarding the safety and mental health of LGBTQIA+ children and adolescents, very little is done to prepare their future teachers to be allies and advocates. As found in "The National School Climate Survey" conducted by GLSEN, LGBTQIA+ students frequently feel unsafe at school because of their gender expression and/or expressed sexual orientation, with more than 85% of students experiencing verbal harassment, 27% of students experiencing physical harassments, and 13% experiencing physical assault (GLSEN, 2016). While secondary education settings do provide some visible school resources for their students, including Gay/Straight Alliances, only three states – New York, Connecticut, and Massachusetts – have LGBTQIA+ alliance clubs/memberships in half of their state's high schools (Parris & Stratford, 2019). Only eight states – California, Nevada, Washington D.C., Florida, Delaware, Vermont, Maine, and Rhode Island – have a Gay/Straight alliance presence in at least 40% of high schools. In perspective, this means that 39 states (including the District of Columbia) have fewer than 39% of high schools with LGBTQIA+ alliance clubs/memberships (Parris & Stratford, 2019).

The presence of allyship and alliances in schools is documented as one of the most consistent ways to improve school climates and academic outcomes for members of the LGBTQIA+ community (Day, Ioverno, & Russell, 2019). However, few if any such groups or presence consistently exists at the elementary or primary education level, leaving a gap in how to address the climate and academic outcomes for members, allies, and future allies of the LGBTQIA+ community in these school settings. Certainly, curricular elements, such as literacy-based efforts with representative texts, are emerging as a resource to promote positive lenses of equity and acceptance. But, the need to "dismantle" the (re)/enforcement of gender dichotomies

DOI: 10.4324/9781003110934-2

and heteronormativity is paramount at the classroom and pedagogical levels, especially in elementary settings where extracurricular support is currently absent. France (2019) establishes that the "moral imperative" of including LGBTQIA+ curriculum as an intentional part of classroom rhetoric is based on the realization that 10% of secondary students and one-in-ten educators in K-12 classrooms identifies as part of the LGBTQIA+ community (France, 2019; CDC, 2016). The "moral imperative" France (2019) refers to is obviously not one of the representations in school settings; it is one of the rhetoric and reliable resources.

GLSEN's "National School Climate" survey, referred to as the "flagship report" on the school experiences of LGBTQIA+ students in schools, has found that LGBTQIA+ students face "unique" and "individualized' challenges when compared to their heterosexual and cisgender, gender-conforming, and gender-presenting counterparts (GLSEN, 2016, p. 2). These experiences are documented as "more hostile" and with "higher rates of bias" in middle grades when compared to high school settings (GLSEN, 2019a). Middle school students were also less likely than high school students to have access to LGTQIA+ school-related resources, including Gay-Straight Alliance organizations, supportive educators, LGBTQIA+-inclusive curricular resources, and inclusive policies GLSEN, 2019a, p. 15). While the GLSEN data do not survey elementary or primary-aged students, there is a trending indication that bullying and discrimination are (1) more prevalent in younger grades/ages and (2) mitigated with less intervention in younger grades/ages. Meyer, Quantz, Taylor, and Peter (2019) further illuminate this trend in their findings that elementary educators are less comfortable discussing LGBTQIA+ issues in classrooms when compared to secondary educators (Meyer et al., 2019, p. 8). Further, elementary educators are found to be less likely to participate in LGBTQIA+ inclusive efforts within school contexts when compared to secondary educators, at a difference of 22%–47%, respectively (p. 8). The reasoning for this resistance and reticence is categorized by Meyer et al. (2019) as "fear-based," pertaining to fear of parents' opposition, legal implications, administration and school board objections, and fear related to job security. In addition to these reasons, more than 38% of elementary educators (e.g., teachers of grades kindergarten through fourth grade) reported that they felt their students were "too young" to discuss LGBTQIA+ topics (p. 8). While discussions of sex and procreation are mature subjects (mature having here the meaning complex, rather than inappropriate), discussions of identity, love, acceptance, empathy, recognition, friendship, advocacy, and allyship are naturally occurring topics among even young children.

Children are not "entities on their way to adulthood" (Steinberg, 2018, p. 5). And this is because such implies that children are unevolved adults, which is harmful and demeaning in its (lack of) appreciation for childhood, even in and by the hands of those who wish to preserve childhood. As Steinberg discusses, childhood is a robust state of being and childhood should not be disregarded – as it often is in positivist views – as a powerless and vulnerable state, save the salvation of adult intervention and passive recipient of adult strategies. Instead, childhood is and should be constructed by helping a child develop a critical consciousness and to "employee their perspectives in solving their problems" (Steinberg, 2018, p. 9). Friendship, love, relationships, families and familial structures, acceptance, collaboration, and so on are problems to be grappled with solved, even at the level of childhood. Thus, there is no room for the argument that children are "too young" and childhood should be safe-guarded from discussions and topics pertinent to the LGBTQIA+ community and the affirmation of all students and their families (Human Rights Campaign . . ., 2021). The understanding of this work is that childhood does not hold the same predilections as adulthood; childhood is unique and is not meant to conform to the social order of adulthood because childhood has its own social order (Steinberg, 2018, pp. 47–48). This work holds with Freire's idea that effective, critical childhood education is that which has a vested interest in the knowledge acquired by children. Further, the consideration of childhood's social order should be determined by the criticality and curiosity of children, not adult phobias.

The reality is that the elementary or primary student who identifies as a member of the LGBTQIA+ community experiences childhood, and elementary school, from a stark and differing vantage from their peers because of the lack of affirmed support within school buildings and the absence of classroom rhetoric that welcomes and supports these students. Laws that prohibit the "promotion of homosexuality" (referred to as "no promo homo" laws) are still in place in six states in the United States at the time of this writing: Alabama, Louisiana, Mississippi, Oklahoma, South Carolina, and Texas (Kosciw, Clark, et al, 2019). Further, both South Dakota and Missouri have in place legislation that prohibits local school districts from having anti-bullying and harassment policies that specifically protect students on the basis of sexual orientation and gender identity (Kosciw, Clark, et al, 2019). As a result, LGBTQIA+ students are more likely to underperform in school, struggle with their own identity and mental health, encounter bullying, and lack support from their peers, teachers, and school communities (Thoreson, 2016). These students consistently describe increased patterns of isolation, exclusion, and marginalization (Thoreson, 2016). As with the antiquated, positivist notion of childhood, schooling, administration, and legislation are vastly outdated, useless, and – as established – harmful. Continuing to perpetuate notions of the twenty-first-century schooling from the tailpipe of the 1973 ban on same-sex marriage is holding back education. Thus, needed are updated considerations and approaches to integrate LGBTQIA+ advocacy, equity, and allyship within classrooms, beginning in elementary classrooms.

The elementary or primary school classroom is not "too early" to see the effects of discrimination, stigmatization, and bullying of LGBTQIA+ students (Kosciw, Clark, et al, 2019; GLSEN & Harris Interactive, 2012). These schools and classrooms are, therefore, not impervious to the integration of social justice advocacy through curriculum and pedagogy to disrupt heteronormativity. In the 2012 partnership study between GLSEN and Harris Interactive Inc., elementary school students were asked to recount their observations and experiences at school regarding bullying and bullying related to gender issues and family diversity. A total of 1,065 elementary students (third, fourth, fifth, and sixth graders) and 1,099 elementary teachers (kindergarten to sixth grade) were surveyed with the intent to speak to the lived experiences of elementary students that precede the bullying, bias, and harassment characteristic of secondary education experiences (GLSEN & Harris Interactive, 2012, p. xv). The findings indicate that 50% of students and teachers hear the term "gay" utilized in a negative context. Forty percent students reported hearing sexist admonishments, such as "boys should do" or "girls should not do" while at school. Though less common, the report found a prevalence of homophobic language in elementary-aged children. But, the homophobic practices go beyond language and dispel the belief that children always misunderstand the language they use and cannot understand the harm or intent. Sixty percent students attribute bullying to their physical attributes, including "being a boy that acts or looks 'too much like a girl or a girl who acts or looks' 'too much like a boy'" (GLSEN & Harris Interactive, 2012, pp. xvi–xvii).

As discussed, the issue – even in elementary or primary setting – is not one of the representations. The GLSEN and Harris Interactive (2012) study found that nearly one in ten elementary students report that they do not conform to traditional gender norms (p. xviii). These students are almost twice as likely to be bullied or made fun of at school (56% versus 33%). This bullying comes in the form of rumors spread about them, cyberbullying via the internet, and even physical harm and compromised safety. Nongender-conforming students share that they are less likely to feel safe at school, and more than 30% of these students do not want to attend school because they feel "unsafe" or "afraid" (p. xviii). From this vantage, it is disheartening to consider that these children do not have resources and advocates within their classrooms that should be safe places for all children.

Elementary school teachers in the GLSEN and Harris Interactive (2012) study shared that while they feel that they do have an individual and professional obligation to ensure feelings of safety and security for all students – including those who identify as members of the LGBTQIA+ community – greater than 50% of these teachers thought a non-gender-conforming student would feel uncomfortable in their schools (p. xix). Greater than 50% of these teachers also felt that a student with a parent who identifies as a member of the LGBTQIA+ community would feel uncomfortable in their schools (p. xix). These teachers share that they are "comfortable" addressing issues of bullying but are not comfortable responding to questions regarding LGBTQIA+ individuals and communities and, as a result, very few reported teaching about LGBTQIA+ families in their classrooms (GLSEN & Harris Interactive, 2012, p. xxi). This could be explained by the lack of professional development that was reported to be provided to teachers on LGBTQIA+ students, families, and resources (p. xxi). Only 37% of surveyed teachers reported that they ever received professional development on gender (including sexism, gender roles, or gender stereotypes) (GLSEN & Harris Interactive, 2012, p. 119). Additionally, only 23% of surveyed teachers reported that they received any professional development on families with LGBTQIA+ parents.

This lack of professional development and training is not exclusively due to a lack of welcoming perspectives in the building, or even at the district level. The GLSEN and Harris Interactive (2012) report found that teachers and administrators are often prepared to be inclusive but meet with resistance often and loudly by other parents. The report states, "both children with LGBT parents and LGBT parents themselves report that they are more likely to be mistreated by other parents than by school personnel" (GLSEN & Harris Interactive, 2012, p. 102). In fact, only 10% of responding teachers opposed the LGBTQIA+ community. This implies that the lack of resources and advocacy LGBTQIA+ students, their families, and allies find in elementary classrooms is imposed upon teachers – rather than brought about by teachers – because of the fear of backlash, a lack of professional development and experience, and/or nonacademic opposition (Meyer et al., 2019; GLSEN & Harris Interactive, 2012).

It feels only natural to suggest that if teachers are not the impetus of the problem, they could be the instrument of the solution. But, navigating the antagonism presented by community stakeholders who are, arguably and on the whole, not professional educators, is daunting and the research supports that this is enough to prevent practicing elementary classroom teachers from implementing LGBTQIA+ representation and advocacy into their curriculum. In order to promote the complete picture of elementary education, school curriculum and pedagogy must embrace resources, literacy, and texts, definitions, vocabulary and terminology, examples, and advocacy of LGBTQIA+ students, families, and allies. The prevalence of data depicting the distressing state of LGBTQIA+ students' lived experiences, alongside the glaring absence of studies that promote concrete steps to solve these issues, illuminates the results found in the those few studies that address this topic: while individuals recognize the importance, they are without the resources to overcome passive compliance. The route to allyship, especially for teachers and education professionals, involves overcoming the systems in place, implying a need to address and instill a queered pedagogical lens during teacher preparation. We turn now to an overview of teacher education and examine the extant presence (or not) of LGBTQIA+ representation in teacher education preparation.

Research shows that children identifying as LGBTQIA+ do so as young as kindergarten (McEntarfer, 2016) and look for allies and adults to talk to, including their teachers. However, teacher education programs are woefully underprepared to address the needs of LGBTQIA+ children as part of their curriculum (Clark, 2010). In our own program, well over 65% of candidates felt that they were either "under-prepared or not at all prepared" for LGBTQIA+ students in their classroom, a percentage that largely reflects other teacher education programs. In our study, this was especially true of the candidates being confident or comfortable in welcoming children who identify as transgender. As teacher educators, it is clear to us that more needs to be done to address this in teacher preparation programs. Indeed, Martino (2013) calls for:

> [N]ot only a special focus on transgender and nonconforming identities in teacher education curricula but also a systematic effort and critical commitment to addressing the very privileging of the hegemonic systems that constrain and curtail a more just politics of gender expression and embodiment within the context of teacher education.
>
> (p. 171)

This lack of inclusionary and anti-oppressive instruction in elementary teacher education programs manifests in the colonizing effects of heteronormativity, especially as it relates to cisgender assumptions of teacher candidates. These assumptions however are rooted in historical perspectives and practices that date back to the origin of teacher preparation in the United States.

Formal teacher preparation programs have been a staple of American education since the 1820s with the establishment of the first "normal schools" in the states of Vermont and Massachusetts. By the early 1900s, almost every major city in the United States had a normal school focused specifically on the art of teaching (Ducharme & Ducharme, n.d.). Over the years, the normal schools evolved into four-year colleges and, later, state universities to meet new regulations and licensure requirements for both the students and the institutions of higher learning. To date, most teacher preparation programs are housed in on-campus teacher education programs or colleges (Ducharme & Ducharme, n.d.), accompanied by asynchronous, online education programs at the undergraduate and graduate degree levels, either associated with state universities or through other for-profit programs, growing daily.

The second area of the field of education that continues to evolve is the identity of teachers in the field and educators in professional education programs. Historically, teaching was once considered a career for men. It was not until the late 1800s that women began to outnumber men in elementary and middle classrooms, and not until the 1970s in many American high schools (Ducharme & Ducharme, n.d.; PBS, n.d.); many of these classroom teachers identified as White, middle-class individuals. Reasons for this include compensation, employment and educational opportunities afforded, and stereotypes about teaching being a feminine profession. In many areas of education, this still holds true and remains the same for teacher candidates who most often identify as middle class, heterosexual, White, and females (Cho & Tersigni, 2014). Similarly, diversity among college faculty, including those in teacher education, has not kept up with the diversity of students although it has increased over the past two decades according to Pew Research Center (Geiger, 2018). As of 2017, three-quarters of all post-secondary faculty members in the United States identified as White. One statistics that is harder to generate is that of the number of teachers, either in the classroom or in high education, that identify as LGBTQIA+. One reason for this is that teachers have always been seen as acting in place of parents when around their students, historically being pushed to appear as having high moral standards not always associated with LGBT communities. For example, as recently as the Cold War, LGBTQIA+ teachers were seen as recruiters for the Communist party, using sex to entice people into joining (Harbeck, 1997). Still today, it has been our experience as educators that many in the field choose to hide their authentic gender and/or sexual identity rather than face being ostracized or harassed.

Despite shifts in the demographics of the teaching profession, an area of teacher education that has remained consistent throughout the years is the content offered in most programs. According to Stengal and Tom (1996), "Traditional teacher education programs are typically marked by three components: foundations of schooling and learning, teaching methodology, and practice teaching" (p. 593). Often included in this curriculum is information on different principles of learning linked to the areas of psychology and philosophy. What has not been incorporated into the education curriculum historically is content that helps prepare new teachers to incorporate issues of diversity, equity, and inclusion and have critical conversations with students that allow them to challenge stereotypes and examine their own identities and ways of thinking. We would argue that without this critical part of the curriculum, teacher educators are failing their students by not fully preparing them to enter diverse classrooms.

Teacher education programs are designed to help teacher candidates gain experience and prepare for their commitment to the education profession. In general, the goals of most teacher preparation programs may include imparting knowledge of the subject matter, pedagogical processes, professional dispositions, and basic knowledge of child psychology to better understand the difficulties faced at different ages and grade levels. Additionally, many teacher preparation programs claim to include aspects of diversity and inclusion needed to sufficiently support students in the classroom but largely define these topics by race, culture, and socioeconomic standing, especially in elementary teacher preparation programs. Indeed, Carpenter and Lee (2010) argue that heteronormativity is taught as a "hidden curriculum" in many teacher education programs. What seems to be missing from the majority of teacher preparation programs is accurate information about LGBTQIA+ issues that "encourage engagement and responsibility and offer practical strategies for making a difference" (Kitchen & Bellini, 2012, p. 210).

Equally concerning are the findings of Robinson and Ferfolja (2010), who found that "pre-service teachers often do not see equality (and social justice issues more generally) as a priority in their learning" (p. 125), often because it is not stressed or missing from their teacher preparation curriculum. Indeed, education students may easily perceive courses with diversity, inclusion, and equity components as just another requirement to be gotten through (Ladson-Billings, 1999) rather than as a critical lens for their content knowledge. This does a great disservice to their future students who are immersed from a young age in expectations of cisgender and heterosexual identities (Kissen, 2002). Yet, as children feel more confident looking inward, questioning their identities, and challenging stereotypes, teacher educators need to reevaluate what is being taught and ask themselves if it is enough to support the needs of preservice teachers today. Indeed, research conducted by Kitchen and Bellini (2012) suggests that teacher education programs must evolve and support preservice teachers as they work to develop a better understanding of LGBTQIA+ issues as well as the obligations and regulations required of teachers to help these students feel safe in schools. To the point, Pallotta-Chiarolli (1999) wrote:

> The officially supported challenge of these prejudices, now labeled "inclusive education," is considered so mainstream that an educator

> is not seen to be fulfilling important pedagogic objectives unless these prejudices are adequately voiced and analyzed. Prejudices such as racism, ethnocentrism, and sexism now generally sit securely within this "safe" category, although it certainly was not always the case and in the 1970s and 1980s early proponents risked all the reactions that are now reserved for the "unsafe-to-challenge" category of prejudices.
>
> (p. 191)

Heteronormativity has historically been a construct fixed in our society, woven into cultural practices, and prevalent in education from elementary grades through institutions of higher learning (McEntarfer, 2016; Blackburn & Clark, 2011). Even today, "[d]espite an already established body of research and scholarship designed to inform policy and practice about the troubling impact of heteronormativity in education settings, heteronormative practices are still prevalent" (Surtees & Gunn, 2010, p. 42). Historically, teacher candidates have viewed classrooms and the field of education in general as an area to ignore or downplay critical issues such as sexual orientation, gender, and race, and research shows us that this has been reinforced in practicum experiences by classroom teachers who do not want to disrupt classroom harmony (Cho & Tersigni, 2014). There is a persistent, yet misguided belief that we must protect elementary-aged students from discussions about racism, identity, and prejudice (Hermann-Wilmarth, 2007). However, research shows us that there is a lack of inclusionary and anti-oppressive instruction in teacher education programs that often manifests in the colonizing effects of heteronormativity, especially as it relates to cisgender assumptions of teacher candidates. This is most prevalent in courses geared toward early childhood and elementary education where the school is often thought of as a space where idealized notions of childhood are nurtured (Allan, Atkinson, Brace, DePalma, & Hemingway, 2008).

The question arises then, when we, as teacher educators, know more needs to be done to educate new and future teachers about LGBTQIA+ issues, why are stereotypes such as boys wear blue and sparkles and pink are only for girls (Ryan, Patraw, & Bednar, 2013) still prevalent in classrooms? When asked, teacher candidates have often expressed that they have had few critical discussions regarding oppression and other social–cultural issues such as race, gender, and sexuality (Cho & Tersigni, 2014) during their teacher preparation programs that help to combat ideals such as this. Moreover, Surtees and Gunn (2010) found that preservice teachers preparing to graduate and move into their own classrooms questioned the need for critical discussions around sexuality and gender with students, even going as far as to label these conversations as "risky" or "dangerous." Fear of disrupting the flow of the classroom or upsetting parents often silences preservice teachers who are just starting their careers regardless of personal views or perceived ability to hold these meaningful conversations. Indeed, many elementary preservice teachers often shy away from any discussion or representation of gender or sexuality that is not heteronormative (Alarcón & Bellows, 2018; Hermann-Wilmarth, 2010) in their classrooms and practicum experiences because they have not been exposed to them in their coursework.

For example, data from a 2014 study conducted by Cho and Tersigni where preservice teachers were asked to teach an anti-oppression lesson to elementary students revealed not only that preservice teachers found convenient reasons to minimize engagement in these discussions with their students but also that fear played a critical role in when and how these types of lessons were taught. Thus, "those who teach teachers must start sharing voices from a range of inclusive classrooms so preservice teachers know this work is possible and so they can see how their students may react to lessons they try" (Ryan et al., 2013, p. 102).

Teacher education programs need to provide students with all information necessary to encourage engagement, inclusivity, and better experiences for students in their classrooms. Kelly and Minnes Brandes (2010) write that although some teacher preparation programs may include the aspects of diversity, these topics "are typically marginalized in the program as a whole" (p. 399). This leads to teachers in the field that feel discomfort discussing development, sexuality, and gender (Gunn, 2008) and often shy away from critical discourse that may decenter heteronormativity in their classrooms and students rather than enforcing it (Atkinson, 2002). Undeniably, social justice discourse is necessary to reinforce to students of all ages that differences are normal, valuable, and a thriving part of our society.

The importance of normalizing and supporting all identities is vital as "one in 500 children is significantly gender-variant or transgender" (Brill & Pepper, 2008, p. 2). Speaking to the need to focus on inclusive education practices at the teacher education program level. However, Macgillivray and Jennings (2008) argue that most programs for teacher educators do not adequately address if they do so at all, LGBT issues in their programs. Further, another study, conducted by Schneider and Dimito (2008), showed that most teachers, 82% of those surveyed, reported having almost no experience with, or exposure to LGBT topics during their teacher education programs.

According to Hermann-Wilmarth (2007), teacher educators need to take responsibility to expand what students are asked to consider. This starts with teacher education. "If preservice teachers have never had opportunities to explore their own homophobia, or the ways that homophobia affects students, the likelihood that they will successfully interrupt the ideological heterosexism of schools seems slim" (p. 349). Yet, to date, little has been enacted in teacher education programs – especially for those candidates seeking endorsement at the primary/elementary level – to educate and encourage those in the program to consider alternatives to traditional ways of thinking and teaching. However, research shows us that providing resources, training, and opportunities for reflection and discussion may impact interactions in the classroom and even improve the school climate (Dowling, Rodger, & Cummings, 2007).

This is supported by work conducted by DePalma and Atkinson (2009a), who completed a UK-based participatory action research project that examined heteronormative processes in primary education over a 28-month period. Data collected from the study shows that participants agreed that the chief obstacle in teaching students and/or addressing topics with students – such as LGBTQIA+ – is the lack of information and resources available to them. Once they had the resources, many reported that just this small step made an impact on students. Another study by Kitchen and Bellini (2012) demonstrated that "an inclusive education . . . requires more than a two-hour workshop. For teacher education to be inclusive, LGBTQ students and curriculum need to be present across all courses" (p. 458). We believe that providing preservice elementary teacher candidates with the knowledge and dispositions to address issues facing LGBTQIA+ youth is imperative and represents a significant gap in the current literature. Our study sought to meet the need by providing participants with the opportunities to consider LGBTQIA+ issues in education and create resources needed to engage and support all students.

It is imperative that teacher preparation programs continue to find better ways to educate and equip future generations of teachers in LGBTQIA+ topics. Providing preservice teachers with experiences, knowledge, and resources to connect with and meet the needs of all students is imperative for them to connect with and understand their students. We are overdue for a queering of the curriculum in teacher preparation programs to help preservice teachers expand their understanding of gender diversity in schools, starting with our youngest students, and the importance of creating safe spaces and developing healthy teaching practices that meet the needs of all students (Brill & Pepper, 2008). Preservice teachers must be afforded the opportunities to develop the instructional methods and tools needed to discuss the issues of race, class, sexuality, gender, etc., throughout their programs (Milner, 2003) to help combat the heteronormative practices historically prevalent in teacher education.

References

Alarcón, J., & Bellows, E. (2018). Class meeting as critical pedagogy: Addressing controversial topics and enacting shared responsibility in elementary social studies education. In S. B. Shear, C. M. Tschida, M. E. Bellows, L. B. Buchanan, & E. Saylor (Eds.), *(Re)imagining elementary social studies: A controversial issues reader*. Charlotte, NC: Information Age Publishing.

Allan, A., Atkinson, E., Brace, E., DePalma, R., & Hemingway, J. (2008). Speaking the unspeakable in forbidden places: Addressing lesbian, gay, bisexual and transgender equality in the primary school. *Sex Education, 8*(3), 315–328. https://doi.org/10.1080/14681810802218395

Atkinson, E. (2002). Education for diversity in a multisexual society: Negotiating the contradictions of discourses. *Sex Education, 2*, 119–132.

Blackburn, M. V., & Clark, C. T. (2011). Analyzing talk in a long-term literature discussion group: Ways of operating within LGBT-inclusive and queer discourses. *Reading Research Quarterly, 46*(3), 222–248.

Brill, S., & Pepper, R. (2008). *The transgender child: A handbook for families and professionals*. Cleis Press.

Brömdal, A., & Davis, I. (2022). The pedagogical possibilities of critically examining gender and sexuality in initial teacher education through the lens of intersex. In *Research Anthology on Inclusivity and Equity for the LGBTQ+ Community* (pp. 303–326). IGI Global.

Cho, C. L., & Tersigni, S. (2014). Teaching for change: Teacher candidates' anti-oppression elementary school lesson plans. *LEARNing Landscapes, 7*(2), 83–100. https://doi.org/10.36510/learnland.v7i2.652

Clark, C. T. (2010). Preparing LGBTQ-allies and combating homophobia in a US teacher education program. *Teaching and Teacher Education, 26*(3), 704–713.

Day, J. K., Ioverno, S., & Russell, S. T. (2019). Safe and supportive schools for LGBT youth: Addressing educational inequities through inclusive policies and practices. *Journal of School Psychology, 74*, 29–43. https://doi.org/10.1016/j.jsp.2019.05.007

DePalma, R., & Atkinson, E. (2009a). "No outsiders": Moving beyond a discourse of tolerance to challenge heteronormativity in primary schools. *British Educational Research Journal, 35*(6), 837–855. Retrieved June 9, 2020, from www.jstor.org/stable/40375617

DePalma, R., & Atkinson, E. (2009b). Editorial: The continuing dialogue about sexualities and schooling. *Sex Education: The Continuing Dialogue about Sexualities and Schooling, 9*(2), 125–127.

Dowling, K., Rodger, S., & Cummings, A. (2007). Exploring attitudes of future educators about sexual minority youth. *Alberta Journal of Educational Research, 53*(4), 401–413.

Ducharme, E. R., & Ducharme, M. D. (n.d.). Teacher education – historical overview, international perspective. *Teachers, teaching, programs, and schools – StateUniversity.Com*. Retrieved April 30, 2021, from https://education.stateuniversity.com/pages/2479/Teacher-Education.html

France, P. E. (2019, May 31). Supporting LGBTQ students in elementary school. *Edutopia*. Retrieved from www.edutopia.org/article/supporting-lgbtq-students-elementary-school

Geiger, A. W. (2018). America's public school teachers are far less racially and ethnically diverse than their students. Pew Research Center.

GLSEN (2016). The 2015 national school climate survey: The experiences of lesbian, gay, bisexual, transgender, and queer youth in our nation's schools. Accessed online at https://www.glsen.org/article/2015-national-school-climate-survey.

GLSEN. (2019a). *2019 National School Climate Survey (executive summary)*. New York, NY: Author.

GLSEN. (2019b). *School climate in California (State snapshot)*. New York, NY: Author.

GLSEN & Harris Interactive. (2012). *Playgrounds and prejudice: Elementary school climate in the United States: A survey of teachers and students*. New York: GLSEN. Retrieved from www.glsen.org/sites/default/files/Playgrounds%20%26%20Prejudice.pdf

Gunn, A. C. (2008). *Heteronormativity and early childhood education: Social justice and some puzzling queries*. Unpublished doctoral dissertation, University of Waikato, Hamilton.

Harbeck, K. M. (1997). *Gay and lesbian educators: Personal freedoms, public constraints*. Malden, MA: Amethyst Press.

Hermann-Wilmarth, J. (2007). Full inclusion: Understanding the role of gay and lesbian texts and films in teacher education classrooms. *Language Arts*, *84*(4), 347–356.

Hermann-Wilmarth, J. (2010). More than book talks: Preservice teachers dialogue after reading gay and lesbian children's literature. *Language Arts*, *87*, 188–198.

Human Rights Campaign Foundation. (2021). LGBTQ definitions for children. *Welcoming Schools*. Retrieved from https://welcomingschools.org/resources/definitions-lgbtq-elementary-school

Kelly, D., & Minnes Brandes, G. (2010). "Social justice needs to be everywhere": Imagining the future of anti-oppression education in teacher preparation. *The Alberta Journal of Educational Research*, *56*(4), 388–402. Retrieved from https://journalhosting.ucalgary.ca/index.php/ajer/article/view/55425

Kissen, R. M. (Ed.). (2002). *Getting ready for Benjamin: Preparing teachers for sexual diversity in the classroom*. Lanham, MD: Rowman & Littlefield Publishers.

Kitchen, J., & Bellini, C. (2012). Making it better for lesbian, gay, bisexual, and transgender students through teacher education: A collaborative self-study. *Studying Teacher Education: Journal of Self-Study of Teacher Education Practices*, *8*(3), 209–225.

Kosciw, J. G., Clark, C. M., Truong, N. L., & Zongrone, A. D. (2020). *The 2019 National School Climate Survey: The experiences of lesbian, gay, bisexual, transgender, and queer youth in our nation's schools*. New York: GLSEN.

Ladson-Billings, G. J. (1999). Chapter 7: Preparing teachers for diverse student populations: A critical race theory perspective. *Review of research in education*, *24*(1), 211–247.

Macgillivray, I. & Jennings, T. (2008). A content analysis exploring lesbian, gay, bisexual, and transgender topics in foundations of education textbooks. *Journal of Teacher Education, 59*(2), 170–188.

Martino, W. (2013). An invaluable resource for supporting transgender, transsexual, and gender non-conforming students in school communities: A review of Supporting transgender and transsexual students in K-12 schools. *Journal of LGBT Youth, 10*(1–2), 169–172.

McEntarfer, H. K. (2016). *Navigating gender and sexuality in the classroom: Narrative insights from students and educators*. New York: Routledge.

Meyer, E. J., Quantz, M., Taylor, C., & Peter, T. (2019). Elementary teachers' experiences with LGBTQ-inclusive education: Addressing fears with knowledge to improve confidence and practices. *Theory into Practice, 58*(1), 6–17. https://doi.org/10.1080/00405841.2018.1536922

Milner, H. (2003). Reflection, racial competence, and critical pedagogy: How do we prepare pre service teachers to pose tough questions? *Race, Ethnicity and Education, 6*(2), 193–208.

Pallotta-Chiarolli, M. (1999). Diary entries from the "teachers' professional development playground". *Journal of Homosexuality, 36*(3–4), 183–205. https://doi.org/10.1300/J082v36n03_12

Parris, B. & Stratford, D. (2019, November 5). *Only 3 states have a gay-straight alliance in over half their schools*. https://www.childtrends.org/blog/only-3-states-have-a-gay-straight-alliance-in-more-than-half-of-their-high-schools

PBS. (n.d.). *PBS online: Only a teacher: Teaching timeline. Only a teacher, Teaching timeline*. Retrieved May 4, 2021, from www.pbs.org/onlyateacher/timeline.html

Robinson, K. H., & Ferfolja, T. (2010). "What are we doing this for?" Dealing with lesbian and gay issues in teacher education. *British Journal of Sociology of Education, 22*(1), 121–133. https://doi.org/10.1080/01425690020030828

Ryan, C. L., & Hermann-Wilmarth, J. M. (2018). *Reading the rainbow: LGBTQ-inclusive literacy instruction in the elementary classroom*. Teachers College Press.

Ryan, C., Patraw, J., & Bednar, M. (2013). Princess boys and pregnant men: Teaching about gender diversity and transgender experiences within an elementary school curriculum. *Journal of LGBT Youth, 10*(1–2), 83–105.

Schneider, M., & Dimito, A. (2008). Educators' beliefs about raising lesbian, gay, bisexual, and transgender issues in the schools: The experience in Ontario. *Journal of LGBT Youth, 5*(4), 49–71.

Steinberg, S. R. (2018). *Kinderculture: The corporate construction of childhood*. New York: Routledge.

Stengal, B, & Tom, A. (1996.) "Changes and Choices inTeaching Methods." In *The Teacher Educator's Handbook*, ed. Frank B. Murray. San Francisco: Jossey-Bass.

Surtees, N., & Gunn, A. (2010). (Re)Marking heteronormativity: Resisting practices in early childhood education contexts. *Australasian Journal of Early Childhood, 35*. https://doi.org/10.1177/183693911003500107

Thoreson, R. (2016, December 7). Like walking through a hailstorm. *Human Rights Watch*. Retrieved from www.hrw.org/report/2016/12/08/walking-through-hailstorm/discriminationagainst-lgbt-youth-us-schools#

3 Multimodal Literacies and LGBTQIA+ Children's Literature

Writing the Rainbow

In recent times, the use of digitally mediated texts, including those used in social media, has provided a platform for addressing social justice issues and bringing public attention to issues of equity and anti-discrimination. From the digital texts and multimodal literacies evident in the *#MeToo, Black Lives Matter, #IrunwithAhmed* movements to name a few, digital communication changes the ways we present, re-present, advocate, and share knowledge individually and internationally (Price-Dennis & Carrion, 2017). Given the omnipresent use of digital and multimodal literacies in our students' lives, we drew from culturally responsive teaching practices (Gay, 2000; Ladson-Billings, 1995; Nieto & Bode, 2008) to engage our students across courses and assignments pertinent to this project. However, as teacher educators, we were cognizant that while our students, were highly competent in traditional print-based literacies, and considered "digital natives" (Smith, Kahlke, & Judd, 2020) in their personal lives, for many, there was a divide between those two worlds. That is, there was a dichotomy between how they used, produced, and consumed digital communication every day, and what they defined as "real" or legitimate applications of literacy, which tended to be more traditionally situated in reading and writing print-based texts. Thus, it was also our responsibility and intent to integrate this dichotomous view to a more unified understanding of digital literac(ies).

In this chapter then, we offer some exemplars from previous research that has drawn from multimodal or digital writing to expand the possibilities for teacher education with and from a social justice lens. We also provide an overview of previous research that has used children's and/or Young Adult (YA) literature to provide mirrors, windows, and sliding glass doors (Byrne, 2021; McNair & Edwards, 2021) to facilitate the acceptance of and advocacy for LGBTQIA+ people. We then turn to how we specifically utilized multimodal writing practices along with picture books to act as a catalyst for operationalizing our student's exploration of topics and issues relevant to the LGBTQIA+ community.

DOI: 10.4324/9781003110934-3

For our purposes, here, we define multimodal literacies as a means of understanding how the integrated use of technology and web-based tools can impact and interact with the social world (Cope & Kalantzis, 2000). Specifically, for literacy and literacy instruction for preservice teachers, we also reflect on research in multimodal literacies and the ways it reconceptualizes and re-envisions what constitutes literacy both for children and for their teachers (Albers, Vasquez, & Harste, 2008; Beach & O'Brien, 2015).

While the term "digital writing" defies a single interpretation, we employ Pandya and Sefton-Green working definition (2021) to "encompass all forms of communication, expression, and creativity that involve digital production" (p. 113). Digital texts then may be seen as integral to the active understanding of and participation in multimodal literacies. As Luke (2008) explains, there are several elements of literacies that come into play as we expand our definition to include:

- a blending of print and digital literacies
- design as a unifying principle across technologies
- a pedagogy pattern on teacher–learner interaction
- focus on youth and technological cultures

Further, we agree with Hull and Katz' (2006) claim that if students of all ages are encouraged to work with technolog(ies) relevant to their daily lives, it may lead to creating a previously unused voice and developing understandings that have yet to be explored. This was certainly the case in the present study. As our students navigated both new and challenging information, they were concomitantly exploring multimodal technologies and the ways of expressing themselves as they created their children's picture books, expository texts, or infographics. This at times tenuous process offered a creative space yet also acted as a constraining force as they sought to re-present the stories or information they wanted to share. However, as we will see later in this volume, in navigating digital texts, they did employ a previously unused medium for sharing their developing understandings of topics relevant to the LGBTIA+ community.

Multimodal Literacies Facilitating Social Justice

Before we provide examples of how teacher educators have utilized digital texts and multimodal literacies to promote social justice, we first need to define the term. It is impossible to discuss social justice in education without first drawing from Freire's seminal work and his concept of *conscientização* which provides a theoretical grounding for reading both the written word and the world that informs them. As the bedrock of critical pedagogical thought, Freire (1970) insists on the examination and understanding of the interconnectedness of ideology, power, and culture. Additionally, Freire speaks to the integral importance of the individual as central to their own liberation as well as the collective fight against oppressive societal constructs – including those in education.

Sorte and Vicentini (2020) argue, "Exploitation, marginalization, poverty, and the perpetuation of inequities around the world are disclosed when education for social justice is prioritized in schools alongside teacher education" (p. 204). Thus for this work, we define educational practices for social justice as those that intentionally utilize a variety of literacies to engage in the deconstruction of societal inequities to reconstruct along with students a more just and equitable world for historically marginalized groups such as the impoverished, or "lower-class," LGBTQIA+, Black, Indigenous, People of Color (BIPOC) women, the differently abled, etc., who have been subjected to hegemonic and discriminatory practices both in society in general and in schools specifically. Thus, the intent is to facilitate opportunities and nurture individual dispositions so that students can engage in participatory work to promote societal change and democratic civic engagement (Picower, 2011; Westheimer & Kahne, 2004).

With "social justice" defined, we situate the production and consumption of digital texts as a potent tool in the fight against inequities. We are including digital writing as a tool of communication under the broader umbrella of multimodal literacies. However, we are also cognizant that the means and affordances of digital communication are also community based and therefore have different uses for different people in times and contexts. As Turner and Hicks (2012) state:

> Digital writing is both local and global, combining elements of multimedia in creative ways to express thoughts and opinions to a real audience that participates in a virtual community of readers and writers. Digital writing is not confined to the classroom corkboard or refrigerator door, and, under the right circumstances, it has the power to influence communities.
>
> (p. 58)

It is in this power "to influence communities" that digital texts, and the use of multimodal literacies have begun to change the approaches to, and engagement in, acts of social justice and liberatory practice both in classrooms and in larger communities.

We turn now to exemplars from the field that provided a model of how teacher educators have utilized multimodal literacies to address issues of social justice. While these examples are not meant to be an exhaustive review, they do provide insights and inspiration for integrating both social justice topics and multimodal literacies into preservice teacher education.

Integrating critical literacy (Luke, 2004; Morrell, 2015), her students' existing social justice concerns, and digital activism (Amin, 2009) led Natalie Amgott (2018) to work with her education students to address local food deserts and the need of the campus food bank for updated marketing and information for its website. Using an approach grounded in restorying (Thomas & Stornaiuolo, 2016) the deficit narratives around food insecurity, Amgott structured a series of sessions to use critical literacy to scaffold her students in researching, storyboarding, and producing a digital text with inclusive hashtags for the campus food bank. By creating a space for her students to explore topics relevant to their lives and community, Amgott also took the knowledge one step further into activism. Student reflections indicated an increase in awareness of the issue, as well as feeling that digital literacy and digital activism helped them feel more empowered and active in addressing social justice issues such as food insecurity.

Similar to how students addressed the needs of their local food bank by creating media to promote awareness, Diane Watt (2019) engaged her preservice elementary education students in critical digital literacy practices using video production as a multimodal outlet. While video production and consumption are ubiquitous in the daily lives of adults and youth, it is still not used to its fullest potential in the elementary classroom. Rather than being a creative modality to explore critical issues, it is often relegated to a banking method (Freire, 1970) of instruction, rather than shared production of knowledge. Ironically, although absent from most mainstream classrooms, even very young children are proficient in creating and sharing songs, drawings, and videos among family members, peers, and online audiences (Vasquez & Branigan Felderman, 2013).

Seeking to address this gap in pedagogy and teacher education with her students, Watts created a multimodal curriculum design project for her preservice teachers to explore both relevant social justice issues important to them while also learning how to utilize video-making as a transformative practice. Some of the topics that students focused on included an anti-bullying awareness campaign, creating nonstereotypical news stories, challenging gender stereotypes in advertisements aimed at children, telling a fairy tale from a nondominant perspective, and writing a personal anthem based on student identities and interests among other interesting projects. By integrating critical pedagogy strategies such as critiquing and questioning existing videos, preservice elementary educators in this study became more adept at successfully integrating critical lenses into their budding use of multimodal videos as tools in transformative practice. Like

Amgott (2018) students, reflections indicated that participants in this study also developed an expanded sense of "what counts" as legitimate literacy practice and how multimodal literacies can serve a multifaceted purpose of integrating digital production and social justice.

Utilizing multimodal literacies and digital texts as transformative practice in teacher preparation is a global endeavor, especially for areas where access to resources, such as technology have not been as readily available as in the Global North. The power of technology to create opportunities, educational access, and more ample pathways for interpersonal and public communication has led to numerous initiatives on the continent of Africa. One such endeavor, the *Cyber Lives Project* (*CLP*), responded to the need to integrate technology into teaching and learning at schools and in institutions of higher education in South Africa (Kajee, 2018). CLP employed three overarching goals:

- to map digital literacy practices across contexts in-and-out-of-school;
- to establish connections with and an understanding of students' digital identity narratives; and
- to consider the implications of digital practices for teaching and learning English

(Kajee, 2018, p. 2)

Leila Kajee (2018) focused her research on examining how students constructed their identities digitally through the multimodal narratives they created in the English classroom. Importantly, given the context and the timing of decolonization efforts in South Africa at the time, Kajee studied preservice English teachers and the process they went through to create digital identities through narratives that evidenced the unrest they were currently living through.

Kajee notes that the political and social backdrop at the time of her study greatly impacted her subjects' narratives. For example, widespread protests and resistance to colonial iconography (not unlike the protests of Confederate monuments in the United States) combined with growing anger over the abysmal graduation rates of Black South African children to White South Africans: 5% of the former compared to over 60% of the latter graduate high school shone a spotlight on racial inequities. Themes of the tensions and social resulting from decolonization efforts were not surprisingly evident in her participants' narratives and digital identities. Students spoke of their frustration and anger over their daily struggles from financial hardships to events of discrimination, as well as feeling "sold out" by the previous generation as they did not believe there was sufficient African voice or influence at the university.

In addition to decolonizing individual students' identities, Kajee sees and calls for these digital literacies to be utilized to decolonize pedagogy and educational spaces as well. She notes that multimodal and digital literacies and practices provide opportunities for students to use their own experiences and voices to act as agents of change. However, this is not limited to the physical classroom, but to digital and virtual spaces as well as we will see with our final exemplar.

Ian O'Byrne (2019) notes that as youths are engaging in their own activism that involves digital media and texts, their teachers, and by extension teacher educators, "need to consider ways in which they can bring these skills, practices, and texts into the classroom" (p. 641). Connecting these actions to digital activism (Yang, 2016; Gerbaudo, 2017) O'Byrne's ethnographic study examined how technology can both resist and/or sometimes reinforce hurtful discourses. As tragic events such as the mass murder at the Mother Emanuel African Methodist Episcopal (AME) Church and the police shooting of Walter Scott brought to the forefront racial injustice, they also witnessed a surge in digital activism and social connections that also found their way into classrooms.

Although O'Byrne did not directly research classrooms or teacher education, his case study of one local activists' use of digital media and texts and the communities' reaction to them has direct implications for classroom practice. He urges teachers to educate, empower, and advocate and to teach in a way that demonstrates how various digital technologies can be used to achieve those objectives by creating networked spaces of like-minded educators. He warns though that these efforts may not be widely accepted and that a risk assessment should be conducted to determine how well digital activism in the English Language Arts (ELA) class and curriculum will be supported by fellow teachers, administrators, parents, and other community stakeholders.

LGBTQIA+ Children's Literature in Teacher Preparation

The inclusion of children's literature in teacher preparation has been a staple in teaching preservice teachers how to create and sustain a literacy-rich environment in their future classrooms. Despite pressures from mandates and scripted curriculum, picture books have been an invaluable resource to engage children in literacy learning (Flores, Vlach, & Lammert, 2019). In addition to being a resource for literacy learning and engagement, picture books have also paved the way for a more racially just, culturally responsive pedagogy and classroom environment (Haddix & Price-Dennis, 2013). Further, children's literature creates opportunities for teachers and students to engage in critical conversations and transformative practices that challenge inequities seen and faced by children in their everyday worlds (Leland, Lewison, & Harste, 2017; Giroux, 1985).

While the use of LGBTQIA+ children's and young adult literature is also slowly making its way into teacher preparation and elementary classrooms, resistance is more likely than acceptance (Blackburn, Clark, & Nemeth, 2015; Blackburn & Clark, 2011). Books with LGBTQIA+ characters or even overtones frequently are placed on challenged or banned book lists in many school districts and/or public libraries (Flood, 2020). To define the related terms, a challenged book (or other media) is one where an attempt to remove or restrict materials or services based on content has been formally lodged. A banned book (or other media) is the result of the removal of materials or services based on content. According to the American Library Association (ALA), there was a 17% increase last year in the number of books targeted for removal from school libraries, with 377 challenges in 2019 and 566 books targeted. Of the top ten most challenged books in 2019, seven were challenged for LGBTQIA+ overtones and/or content.

While long-standing research on the importance of representation and interaction between reader and text (i.e., Rosenblatt, 1938/1985; Sims, 1983) is beginning to be reflected in racially representative decolonizing children's literature (Thomas, 2016) that is not the case for children's literature featuring LGBTQIA+ characters or themes.

As Möller (2020) notes, while the presence of LQBTQIA+ children's literature is a rare occurrence on the typical classroom bookshelf, resistance to its inclusion is pervasive. In a review of 23 studies of preservice teachers or practicing teacher responses to LGBTQIA+ children's literature, Möller found that resistance to the topic and/or its appropriateness in elementary classrooms far outweighed legitimate engagement and response to the texts themselves. Indeed, in many of the studies she reviewed (e.g., Williams, 2002; Hermann-Wilmarth, 2010) debates and protests related to the topic rather than the content of the stories themselves dominated the discussions.

In findings like we encountered in the present study, most teachers agreed that while discussing diversity generally including gender roles and stereotypes were appropriate, discussions of sexual orientation were not. Many preservice or practicing teachers justified not using LGBTQIA+ inclusive books based on their beliefs that such issues were inappropriate for young children, that community member or stakeholder protests could ensue, or that they were not confident in their ability to address LGBTQIA+ issues competently. Of all these factors, however, the fear or anticipation of negative caregiver reaction to the picture books seemed the most prevalent as a cause for resistance. For example, Martino & Cumming-Potvin (2018) noted, "a recurrent theme [of] fear, mindfulness, or cautiousness in relation to the surveillance of the parental community" (p. 314).

While resistance and heteronormative narratives have and do present challenges to the inclusion of LGBTQIA+ children's literature in preservice teacher education and elementary classrooms, research has also demonstrated that understanding, capacity, and even advocacy can be developed. Returning to Rudine Sims Bishop's (1990) approach to literature as windows, mirrors, and sliding glass doors, utilizing LGBTQIA+ children's literature facilitates students who identify, and/or those with LGBTQIA+ families, to see their lives reflected while giving other students windows that see beyond stereotypes and biases. Moreover, it gives teachers the opportunity to resist heteronormativity and to provide the doorway to inclusivity and allyship within the classroom and larger community. However, before this can take place, preservice and practicing teachers need to have the scaffolding and support to explore these texts themselves.

Yet as some teacher educators have found, even with the best of intentions, this may be easier said than done. For example, Ahmed and Ali (2020) forthrightly share their own experiences and what they termed "missed opportunities" to engage preservice teachers in critical discussions using LGBTQIA+ children's literature, namely, *Pride: Harvey Milk and the Story of the Rainbow Flag* (Sanders, 2018). Unprepared for the vehement responses to her questions of how this book might relate to an interdisciplinary approach to literacy and social studies, Ahmed recollects

> "feeling rattled and concerned about LGBTQ-identified pre-service teachers and how they might feel about their classmates' resistance to celebrating the LGBTQ fight for equality; [and] also thinking about elementary students with two moms or two dads."
>
> (p. 69)

While she reminded her students that LGBTQ rights were protected by law, she remembers being unable to truly engage her students past their resistance.

In reimagining a different outcome, Ahmed addresses three areas where she might have better facilitated the discussion before, during, and after reading. Prior to reading the book, Ahmed reflects that she might first considered the juxtaposition of what she considered "controversial" as a progressive educator and what might seem controversial to her students. Second, she reflects that asking questions about the book before its pedagogical use would have better supported her students. Finally, taking a strong stance of allyship while also not being dismissive of her students' concerns, might be articulated in asking open-ended questions such as:

- Would you read this book with students – why or why not?
- For which students might this text be an important "mirror," one that reflects their lived experiences?

- For which students might this text be an important "window" or "sliding glass door" into a world that is different from their own?
- How can literature be used to teach about recent/current events?
- What might you do if you (personally, culturally, religiously, politically) disagree with current law, policy, and/or practice that comes up in your classroom?

(p. 72)

It is instructive for teacher educators to note that simply providing exposure to LGBTQIA+ children's literature may not suffice, without also modeling and exploring pedagogical practices.

Similar conclusions were drawn in a study with preservice teachers in the Midwestern United States, an area known for conservative Christian values, Crawley (2020) decided to provide his students with experiences he found lacking in his teacher preparation program. Namely, he decided to scaffold critical conversations utilizing children's literature – including LGBTQIA+ picture books with his students. He also assisted them in writing rationales and role-playing responses to stakeholders who might question the use of what they might perceive as controversial materials in the classroom. While his students appreciated the time to explore various "windows and mirrors," as well as the focus on a rationale rather than a defense of curricular and pedagogical choices, Crawley importantly notes:

> Asking the pre-service teachers to consider stakeholder responses assumes they will have actually used the texts in their classrooms. Although I shared with the pre-service teachers books, they could use as windows and mirrors followed by how to consider and respond to potential stakeholders, I did not explicitly show them how such books might be read to and discussed with youth.
>
> (p. 72)

Crawley continued with recommendations for scaffolding questions and for providing preservice teachers with the space for discussion not only of the books but how to use them in the classroom to promote inclusivity. While certainly a challenge, it is not an insurmountable goal for teachers and teacher educators.

For example, in an ongoing study with elementary and middle school teachers, Ryan and fellow researchers (2021) created a virtual LGBTQ-inclusive book club. Thirty teachers from ten states enrolled in an online club where each month they read and discussed a different book. Members then met twice a month via Zoom for discussions. In the first of the two monthly meetings, the participants focused on the book and their reactions to it, while the second meeting explored the pedagogical possibilities for each text, including creating multimodal text sets with other related books or materials. While the results of this study have not yet been finalized, early findings indicate that book club members have successfully created an engaging and supportive community. They have also met to work on integrating LGBTQIA+ inclusive literature into their classrooms. Turning from these examples of the challenges and affordance of utilizing LGBTQIA+ children's literature in teacher education, now we describe our own experiences with employing multimodal literacies and LGBTQIA+ literature with preservice teacher candidates.

Writing the Rainbow With Our Teacher Candidates

In conceptualizing our approach to this study, we knew it would be important to provide a space for preservice teacher candidates to explore and engage with LGBTQIA+ inclusive topics, issues, and texts. Concomitantly, we also wanted to incorporate multimodal literacies and digital texts not only to meet the standards of the courses but also to provide opportunities to experiment with pedagogical approaches for their future classrooms. On both fronts, we encountered both resistance and uncertainty regarding our students' beliefs in their efficacy. While we will discuss our methodology in greater detail in subsequent chapters, we provide here an overview of the mentor texts and digital resources we provided our students as they began their work.

One of the first steps we took was to assemble a text set of LGBTQIA+ inclusive children's picture books that could facilitate exploration of topics relevant to the LGBTQIA+ community and act as mentor texts for the genre of narrative children's literature. Similarly, we also gathered examples of infographics and expository texts for students who might want to take a more informational approach. An example of such text sets is shown in Table 3.1.

Similar to the approach taken by Crawley (2020), the books were placed around the classroom on consecutive days of class so that students could explore each book and then discuss what they thought of them in small groups. In the English Language Arts class, select books were also modeled as read-alouds and discussed as a whole group. Not surprisingly perhaps, and reflecting occurrences in studies cited previously, the topics of the discussions frequently shifted from the content of each book to the appropriateness (or not) of sharing these books with elementary students and concerned conversation about the parental or administrative reactions if they did. Despite the resistance and worries regarding how and when to use these texts in their classrooms, the students did draw inspiration from them for their own stories.

Table 3.1 LGBTQIA+ Text Sets

Picture Books	*Expository Texts/Infographics*
Sparkle Boy Newman, L., & Mola, M. (2017). Sparkle boy. Lee & Low Books Incorporated.	**Making Your GSA Inclusive Of Black LGBTQ+ Students** www.glsen.org/sites/default/files/2021-06/GLSEN_GSA_Inclusive_Black_LGBTQ%2B_Students_Resource.pdf
A Day in the Life of Marlon Bundo Twiss, J., & Bundo, M. (2018). Last Week Tonight with John Oliver Presents a Day in the Life of Marlon Bundo. United States: Chronicle Books LLC.	**No Name-Calling Week Social Media Graphics** www.glsen.org/activity/no-came-calling-week-social-share-graphics
Being Jazz: My Life as a (Transgender) Teen Jennings, J. (2017). Being Jazz: My life as a (transgender) teen. Ember.	**10 Back to School Tips for LGBTQ+ Students** www.glsen.org/sites/default/files/2019-12/GLSEN_Back_to_School_Tips_Resource_2019.pdf
And Tango Makes Three Richardson, J., & Parnell, P. (2015). And Tango makes three. Simon and Schuster.	**Fact Sheets and Infographics** www.thetaskforce.org/category/fact-sheets-infographics/
The Bravest Knight who ever Lived Errico, D. J. (2019). The bravest knight who ever lived. Schiffer Publishing Limited.	**Get the Facts about Trans Youth** www.lgbtmap.org/file/Advancing%20Acceptance%20Infographic%20FINAL.pdf
Julian is a Mermaid. Love, J. (2018). Julian is a Mermaid. Somerville, MA: Candlewick Press.	**Understanding Gender Identities** www.thetrevorproject.org/resources/article/understanding-gender-identities/
Introducing Teddy Walton, J. (2016). Introducing Teddy: A gentle story about gender and friendship. Bloomsbury Publishing USA.	**Guide to Being an Ally to Transgender and Nonbinary Youth** www.thetrevorproject.org/wp-content/uploads/2021/07/Guide-to-Being-an-Ally-to-Transgender-and-Nonbinary-Youth.pdf
Pride: The Story of Harvey Milk and the Rainbow Flag Sanders, R. (2018). Pride: The story of Harvey Milk and the rainbow flag. Random House Books for Young Readers.	**Our Children** https://pflag.org/sites/default/files/OUR%20CHILDREN_PFLAG National_FINAL.pdf
When Aidan Became a Brother Lukoff, K. (2019). When Aidan became a brother. Lee & Low Books.	**The Genderbread Person** www.genderbread.org/

Throughout subsequent class meetings, our students met in small groups to brainstorm their topics and, as we will discuss in more detail in subsequent chapters, utilized the Queer Critical Media Literacies framework (Van Leent & Mills, 2018) to assist them in their research. Once the students had decided on issues relevant to the LGBTQIA+ community and having met with representatives from the LGBT community center, they began their research into the topic and began to think about how to translate the information into stories and/or infographics age-appropriate for elementary students. As one candidate reflected:

> Writing the book itself was interesting. Trying to decide on a topic that was interesting to me but not too complex for a child to understand was hard. I ended up deciding on gender stereotypes. The storyline was a little hard to figure out but was easy once a general idea was formed.

Many students also sought out other LGBTQIA+ inclusive picture books and/or expository texts to utilize as models or mentor texts as we had demonstrated during the read-aloud and in the displayed text sets. Once the students had an idea in place, we encouraged them to work collaboratively in small groups to storyboard their projects and to research various free (or low-cost) ways to digitally produce their books. We also gave students the option of creating a "hard copy" and/or hand-drawn version and then digitizing the final product through photographs and slide shows such as Google Slides or PowerPoint.

From Idea to Digital Text

Although many of our students considered themselves to be "digital natives," they also found translating their stories into digital texts to be more difficult than they originally had thought it would be. Many of the challenges stemmed from adapting their works to fit the parameters and images available to them on story creator websites or applications such as *Storybird* (www.storybird.com), *Book Bildr* (www.bookbildr.com), or *Story Jumper* (www.storyjumper.com). While these are just a small selection of available digital book creation sites, they were the most prevalently used. Students who elected to create infographics or expository texts, however, reported a smoother process using sites such as *Canva* (www.canva.com). It should be noted as well that given the various access to technology that was available to our students in their homes, some class time was designated as a "workshop" where students could work on their projects, collaborate with each other, and receive feedback and assistance from their instructors.

Aside from being of pragmatic use, these workshop sessions also facilitated rich discussions as students worked together to try and make sure their projects avoided stereotypes and included diverse representations. It also allowed students to work through some of their own concerns about addressing LGBTQIA+ inclusivity in their future classrooms in a more informal and thus "safer" context than in whole group discussions.

Whatever the form their picture books or informative texts/infographics took, most students reported gaining expertise and a greater sense of self-efficacy in using multimodal literacies throughout the project. Aside from the content that they struggled with to varying degrees, almost all students reported that they would use creating narrative or informative texts with their own future students, and as discussed previously here, many say the affordances for social justice that digital texts could produce given the ease of sharing across multiple platforms.

In this chapter, we briefly reviewed extant literature in multimodal literacies, digital texts, and LGBTQIA+ children's literature to provide exemplars of how they might be used to promote awareness and understanding of social justice issues including those relevant to LGBTQIA+ children, their families, and the larger community. In the next chapter, we provide a more in-depth look at the theories and methods utilized in this study.

References

"Top 100 Most Banned and Challenged Books: 2010–2019", American Library Association, September 9, 2020. http://www.ala.org/advocacy/bbooks/frequentlychallengedbooks/decade2019 (Accessed January 19, 2022) Document ID: ed7826dc-f0a5-4e0b-80cc-5d2d0d448986

Ahmed, K. S., & Ali, N. (2020). What do you do when you don't know how to respond? Supporting pre-service teachers to use picture books to facilitate difficult conversations. *Occasional Paper Series 2020* (44). Retrieved from https://educate.bankstreet.edu/occasional-paper-series/vol2020/iss44/8

Amgott, N. (2018). Critical Literacy in# DigitalActivism: Collaborative Choice and Action. *International Journal of Information and Learning Technology*, *35*(5), 329–341.

Albers, P., Vasquez, V. M., & Harste, J. C. (2008). A classroom with a view: Teachers, multimodality, and new literacies. *Talking Points*, *19*(2), 3–13.

Amin, R. (2009). The empire strikes back: social media uprisings and the future of cyber activism. *Kennedy School Review*, *10*, 64–67.

Beach, R., & O'Brien, D. (2015). Fostering students' science inquiry through app affordances of multimodality, collaboration, interactivity, and connectivity. Reading & Writing Quarterly, 31(2), 119–134.

Blackburn, M. V., & Clark, C. T. (2011). Analyzing talk in a long-term literature discussion group: Ways of operating within LGBT-inclusive and queer discourses. *Reading Research Quarterly*, *46*(3), 222–248.

Blackburn, M. V., Clark, C. T., & Nemeth, E. A. (2015). Examining queer elements and ideologies in LGBT-themed literature: What queer literature can offer young adult readers. *Journal of Literacy Research*, *47*(1), 11–48.
Byrne, C. (2021). Mirrors, windows, and sliding glass doors: LGBTIQA+ perspectives. *Synergy*, *19*(2).
Cope, B., & Kalantzis, M. (2006). From literacy to 'multiliteracies': Learning to mean in the new communications environment. *English Studies in Africa*, *49*(1), 23–45.
Crawley, S. A. (2020). If I knew then what I do now: Fostering pre-service teachers' capacity to promote expansive and critical conversations with children's literature. *Occasional Paper Series 2020* (44). Retrieved from https://educate.bankstreet.edu/occasional-paper-series/vol2020/iss44/12
Flood, A. (2020, April 21.). LGBTQ children's books face record bans in US libraries. *The Guardian*. https://www.theguardian.com/books/2020/apr/21/us-libraries-say-lgbtq-children-books-most-calls-for-bans-last-year-alex-gino-george
Flores, T. T., Vlach, S. K., & Lammert, C. (2019). The role of children's literature in cultivating preservice teachers as transformative intellectuals: A literature review. *Journal of Literacy Research*, *51*(2), 214–232.
Freire, P. (1970). *Pedagogy of the oppressed*. New York: Continuum.
Gay, G. (2000). *Culturally responsive teaching: Theory, research, and practice*. New York, NY: Teachers College Press.
Gerbaudo, P. (2017). From cyber-autonomism to cyber-populism: An ideological history of digital activism. *TripleC: Communication, Capitalism & Critique*, *15*(2), 477–489.
Giroux, H. A. (1985). Teachers as transformative intellectuals. *Social Education*, *49*, 376–379.
Haddix, M., & Price-Dennis, D. (2013). Urban fiction and multicultural literature as transformative tools for preparing English teachers for diverse classrooms. *English Education*, *45*(3), 247–283.
Hermann-Wilmarth, J. M. (2010). More than book talks: Preservice teacher dialogue after reading gay and lesbian children's literature. *Language Arts*, *87*(3), 188–198.
Hull, G. A., & Katz, M. L. (2006). Crafting an agentive self: Case studies of digital storytelling. *Research in the Teaching of English*, 43–81.
Kajee, L. (2018). Teacher education students engaging with digital identity narratives. *South African Journal of Education*, *38*(2), 1–9.
Ladson-Billings, G. (1995). Toward a theory of culturally relevant pedagogy. *American Educational Research Journal*, *32*, 465–491.
Luke, A. (2004). Two takes on the critical. In B. Norton & K. Toohey (Eds.), *Critical pedagogies and language learning* (pp. 21–31). Cambridge: Cambridge University Press.
Luke, A. (2008, May). *Digital innovation in schooling: Policy efficacy, youth cultures and pedagogical change* (Discussion Paper). QUT Digital Repository: http://eprints.qut.edu.au/
Martino, W., & Cumming-Potvin, W. (2016). Teaching about sexual minorities and "princess boys": A queer and trans-infused approach to investigating

LGBTQ-themed texts in the elementary school classroom. *Discourse: Studies in the Cultural Politics of Education, 37*(6), 807–827.

Martino, W., & Cumming-Potvin, W. (2018). Transgender and gender expansive education research, policy and practice: reflecting on epistemological and ontological possibilities of bodily becoming. *Gender and Education, 30*(6), 687–694.

McNair, J. C., & Edwards, P. A. (2021). The lasting legacy of rudine sims bishop: Mirrors, windows, sliding glass doors, and more. *Literacy Research: Theory, Method, and Practice, 70*(1), 202–212. https://doi.org/10.1177/23813377211028256

Möller, K. J. (2020). Reading and responding to LGBTQ-inclusive children's literature in school settings: Considering the state of research on inclusion. *Language Arts, 97*(4), 235–251.

Morrell, E. (2015). *Critical literacy and urban youth: Pedagogies of access, dissent, and liberation*. New York, NY: Routledge.

Nieto, S., & Bode, P. (2008). *Affirming diversity: The sociopolitical context of multicultural education* (5th ed.). Boston, MA: Allyn & Bacon.

O'Byrne, W. I. (2019). Educate, empower, advocate: Amplifying marginalized voices in a digital society. *Contemporary Issues in Technology and Teacher Education, 19*(4), 640–669.

Pandya, J. Z., & Sefton-Green, J. (2021). Reconceptualizing the teaching and learning of digital writing. *Theory into Practice, 60*(2), 113–115.

Picower, B. (2011). Resisting compliance: Learning to teach for social justice in a neoliberal context. *Teachers College Record, 113*(5), 1105–1134.

Price-Dennis, D., & Carrion, S. (2017). Leveraging digital literacies for equity and social justice. *Language Arts, 94*(3), 190.

Rosenblatt, L. M. (1938/1995). *Literature as exploration* (5th ed.). New York, NY: Modern Language Association of America.

Ryan, C. L. (2021). Reading the K-8 rainbow: A virtual, LGBTQ-inclusive children's literature book club for elementary and middle school teachers. *Journal of Children's Literature, 47*(1), 145–148.

Sims, R. (1983). Strong Black girls: A ten year old responds to fiction about Afro-Americans. *Journal of Research and Development in Education, 16*(3), 21–28.

Smith, E. E., Kahlke, R., & Judd, T. (2020). Not just digital natives: Integrating technologies in professional education contexts. *Australasian Journal of Educational Technology, 36*(3), 1–14.

Sorte, P. B., & Vicentini, C. (2020). Educating for social justice in a post-digital era. *Revista Praxis Educacional, 16*(39), 199–216.

Thomas, E. E. (2016). Stories still matter: Rethinking the role of diverse children's literature today. *Language Arts, 94*(2), 112–119.

Thomas, E. E., & Stornaiuolo, A. (2016). Restorying the self: Bending toward textual justice. *Harvard Educational Review, 86*(3), 313–338.

Turner, K. H., & Hicks, T. (2012). "That's not writing": Exploring the intersection of digital writing, community literacy, and social justice. *Community Literacy Journal, 6*(1), 55–78.

Van Leent, L., & Mills, K. (2018). A queer critical media literacies framework in a digital age. *Journal of Adolescent & Adult Literacy, 61*(4), 401–411.

Vasquez, V., & Branigan Felderman, C. (2013). *Technology and critical literacy in early childhood.* New York, NY: Routledge.

Watt, D. (2019). Video production in elementary teacher education as a critical digital literacy practice. *Media and Communication, 7*(2), 82–99.

Westheimer, J., & Kahne, J. (2004). What kind of citizen? The politics of educating for democracy. *American Educational Research Journal, 41*(2), 237–269.

Williams, S. (2002). Reading Daddy's Roommate: Preservice teachers respond to a controversial text. *New Advocate, 15*(3), 231–236.

Yang, G. (2016). Narrative Agency in Hashtag Activism: The Case of #BlackLives Matter. *Media and Communication, 4*(4), 13–17.

Children's Literature Cited

Errico, D. J. (2019). *The bravest knight who ever lived.* Atglen, PA: Schiffer Publishing Limited.

Jennings, J. (2017). *Being Jazz: My life as a (transgender) teen.* Toronto, ON: Ember.

Love, J. (2018). *Julian is a mermaid.* Somerville, MA: Candlewick Press.

Lukoff, K. (2019). *When Aidan became a brother.* New York: Lee & Low Books.

Newman, L., & Mola, M. (2017). *Sparkle boy.* New York: Lee & Low Books Incorporated.

Richardson, J., & Parnell, P. (2015). *And Tango makes three.* New York: Simon and Schuster.

Sanders, R. (2018). *Pride: The story of Harvey Milk and the rainbow flag.* New York: Random House Books for Young Readers.

Twiss, J., & Bundo, M. (2018). *Last week tonight with John Oliver presents a day in the life of Marlon Bundo.* New York: Chronicle Books LLC.

Walton, J. (2016). *Introducing Teddy: A gentle story about gender and friendship.* London: Bloomsbury Publishing.

4 Challenging Teacher Candidate's Heteronormative Assumptions

Our Theoretical Approach and Methodology

This study began with an answer to a university-wide call for intramural funding to improve undergraduate interdisciplinary research writing. While we were eager to assist our students in sharpening their prowess in writing, we saw this as an opportunity to address what we were seeing as a larger area of concern – the almost complete lack of inclusion of the LGBTQIA+ community in discussions and pedagogical decisions related to diversity, equity, and culturally sustaining practice in our teacher preparation programs. Moreover, when I (Judith) attempted to include children's literature centered on LGBTQIA+ individuals and experiences, it was met with pronounced resistance by my preservice teacher candidates. With these concerns forefront in our minds, we decided to center our response to the writing initiative on combating heteronormativity and cisgender assumptions with our preservice elementary teacher candidates.

As mentioned prior, this study took place in the College of Education at a large urban university in the Southeastern United States. The research team for the larger study was comprised of five cisgender females, one of whom identified as a lesbian. Two members were tenured faculty members, one was an untenured senior lecturer, and two were (at the time) doctoral candidates. While the grant we received focused on interdisciplinary collaboration, we do not include data from the courses in Women's Studies for two reasons. The first is that we focus here on facilitating allyship with elementary teachers, and there were no preservice teachers enrolled in the women's studies courses. The second reason pertains more to student dispositions toward the topics at hand. The students enrolled in the women's studies' gender and sexuality courses were necessarily there as either part of their program of study or were taking the course as an elective. Simply put, they were generally not resistant to exploring the issues of gender and sexuality within the context of the college undergraduate classroom. Nor did they share the concerns of our preservice candidates of addressing LGBTQIA+ issues in the at worst, potentially hostile, and at best, the

DOI: 10.4324/9781003110934-4

taciturn atmosphere of elementary classrooms in a conservative part of the United States.

The authors of this text taught or assisted in two different courses (Instructional Technology and PK-6 English Language Arts Methods) over two semesters, equating to one academic year. Seventy-three preservice candidates participated in the study over the course of two semesters. They ranged in age from 21 to 45, although the majority were between 21 and 27 and would be considered "traditional" full-time students. Of those reporting demographic data in a prestudy survey, 34% identified as Black, 12% identified as Latinx, and 54% identified as White. About 100% were identified/assigned as female at birth (AFAB). However, one student identified as male, and one identified as nonbinary. The vast majority identified as cisgender females. Additionally, while many candidates felt they were accepting of lesbian, gay, or bisexual individuals, less than a third felt that way about transgender or nonbinary individuals. Perhaps not surprisingly, given the lack of inclusion of LGBTQIA+ as a component of diversity in the program curriculum, most students in both courses reported that they did not believe they were prepared to address inequities or issues faced by LGBTQIA+ children or their caregivers in their future classrooms. Nor did they believe that they would independently or proactively include topics or materials related to the LGBTQIA+ community in their future classrooms.

Theoretical Framework

To build upon theories that students were already familiar with within our program, our initial approach sought to utilize tenets of intersectionality (Crenshaw, 1991) culturally relevant pedagogy or CRP, (Ladson-Billings, 2006), and critical literacies (Morrell, 2008; Janks, 2017 ; Thomas, Bean-Folkes, & Coleman, 2020), to frame disparate positioning of gender and sexuality using a critical framing of what was positioned as normative or unchallenged. We hoped that the nexus of these three complementary frameworks would be both familiar and challenging for our students. However, although these theories contributed to the foundation a firm theoretical footing for students and faculty alike, it soon became apparent that our framework was not wholly useful in addressing the oppression and discrimination LGBTQIA+ children face from teachers and schools without drawing some incomplete and potentially problematic parallels.

For example, while Crenshaw's work in intersectionality has addressed various intersections of oppression including gender, it is somewhat limited to cisgender experiences as originally conceived. Culturally relevant pedagogy (CRP) has largely centered on the nexus of race and culture as points of pedagogical focus. Similarly, critical literacies, and more recently, restoried critical literacies (Thomas, Bean-Folkes, & Coleman, 2020) have historically focused on race, culture, and social class as sites of struggle and oppression. In utilizing culturally relevant pedagogy and critical literacies as a starting point with students, our intent was not to decenter race, culture, and social class, but rather to illustrate how gender and sexuality operate as points of discrimination, just as race, culture, and class have historically (Aronson & Laughter, 2018). Indeed as Keenan (2012) argues, "despite concerns about its provocative nature, the race-sexual orientation analogy has been drawn by African-Americans at the center of struggles for civil rights and who themselves have experienced racial discrimination" (p. 1231). Moreover, Keenan (2012) situates constructions of race, gender, and sexuality, as early European concepts colored by the sixteenth- and seventeenth-century geographical exploration, and by the eighteenth-, nineteenth-, and twentieth-century pseudo-scientific discourses that have continued to influence current discussions of same-sex marriage and in assumptions about both racialized and homosexualized bodies.

Specifically, Keenan (2012) posits "the relationship between race and sexual orientation is not merely analogous. Rather, the socially constructed categories of race and sexuality are inseparable, and sexual orientation – at least as it appears in current debates – is structured on similar lines. Ultimately . . . racial thinking marks homosexual bodies" (p. 1243). Similarly, Somerville (2000) argues that it is "not merely a historical coincidence that the classification of bodies as either 'homosexual' or 'heterosexual' emerged at the same time that the United States was aggressively constructing and policing the boundary between 'black' and 'white' bodies" (p. 3). Moreover, we contend that in addition to functioning as points of discrimination, biased, or stereotypical views on gender, sexuality, and race also function as points of *education*. Enciso (2007) speaks to this:

> I assume that of the cultural resources we have at hand for the production of knowledge, one of these – in its many forms – is racism. In other words, racism is a source of knowledge for everyone living in the United States. . . . I also assume that without exception, the cultural artifacts, concepts, and forms of mediation circulating and brought into action for making meaning in U.S. schooling are associated with contemporary and historical forms of racism, sexism, heterosexism, and ableism.
>
> (p. 51)

That is, beyond being evidenced as a by-product of a society enmeshed in discriminatory practices and pedagogy, the discrimination itself is a source of meaning-making and knowledge production. Thus, it is vital to counter that insidious knowledge production with those rooted in equity and inclusion. Given that institutions of higher education also function as sites of social and knowledge reproduction ultimately reflected in both public and private PK-12 schools, we renew the call that educational research must identify strategies for supporting LGBTQIA+ youth in these potentially hegemonic educational contexts.

Indeed, as with much in education from primary school to postgraduate study, if not explicitly addressed and made explicit in the curriculum, stereotypes, biases, and past experiences may become the default lens from which candidates view the world. Similar to the ways that unchecked whiteness will oppress students of color, heteronormativity enacts hegemony. For example, in speaking to White resistance to addressing structural inequalities, Christine Sleeter (2001) wrote:

> White preservice students interpret social change as meaning almost any kind of change except changing structural inequalities, and many regard programs to remedy racial discrimination as discriminatory against Whites. White preservice students tend to use colorblindness as a way of coping with fear and ignorance.
>
> (p. 95)

We argue here that more than just being analogous to "colorblindness" as a stance negating oppression related to race, heteronormativity, and cisgender assumptions are social constructions that operate to distinguish normative bodies from those denied legitimacy. Similar to the ways that White people have been conditioned to avoid talking about race to deny inherent structural racism (Tolbert, 2019), straight, cisgender individuals are "imbued . . . to expect heterosexuality" (McEntarfer, 2016, p. 38), which then leads to the perpetuation of a rigid, socially constructed definition of gender and sexuality. Drawing from intersectionality, we also acknowledge here the particular risk encountered by queer students of color who face multiple aspects of jeopardy. Brockenbrough (2015), points to "the bodies of queer students of color [who] are already marked by crisis-oriented discourses on youth of color, queer youth, immigrant youth, poor youth, and other constituencies to which they belong that are considered at risk" (p. 28). Given that the majority of elementary school teachers are still White, middle-class, cisgender women, and the populations they teach are increasingly representative of BIPOC communities (La Salle, Wang, Wu, & Rocha Neves, 2020), the need for an approach to teacher preparation that draws from critical race theory, queer theories, and critical literacies are increasingly evident.

In the context of teaching and teacher education, Aronson and Laughter (2020) report that "schools historically have contributed to silencing queer students by firing teachers or creating legislation limiting curriculum and sexuality education" (p. 10). If discussed in social foundations of education courses at all, textbooks either exclude LGBTQIA+ content or perhaps worse, reinscribe "negative or stereotypical representations" (MacGillivray & Jennings, 2008, p. 171). LGBTQIA+ identities are also often placed in the same contexts as suicide, depression, or sexually transmitted disease, which reifies the identities of these students as victims or at-risk youth in need of protection or therapeutic intervention, rather than as holistic and healthy identities (Payne & Smith, 2011).

What is needed then is a queering of teacher preparation. As argued by Zacko-Smith and Smith (2013), it cannot be simply the purview of teachers who identify as LGBTQIA+ to be the tokenized standard bearers of queer theory. Teacher preparation programs should also minimally provide their candidates with an understanding of queer theory and how it relates to pedagogy. Thus, in taking up that call, we draw from an expanded intersectional approach to critical literacies, CRP, and the theoretical lens of queered pedagogy to encourage students to read, and in our case, write, through the perspective of queer theory (Jagose, 1996; Miller, 2015; Simon et al., 2018; Blackburn & Clark, 2011). As defined by Matthew Thomas-Reid (2018):

> Queer pedagogy draws on the lived experience of the queer, wonky, or non-normative as a lens through which to consider educational phenomena. Queer pedagogy seeks to both uncover and disrupt hidden curricula of heteronormativity as well as to develop classroom landscapes and experiences that create safety for queer participants [online].

Heather McEntarfer (2016) extends this idea by positing, "queer pedagogy asks both students and teachers to look inward." It asks us all to be open to a "reflexive and tentative journey into the unknown and unexamined "differences and oppressors within" (Bryson & de Castell, 1993, p. 300). We also consider how a queer lens contextualizes childhood, and by extension, educating a child. As constructed in a heteronormative tradition, the discourse of childhood innocence is selectively applied and used to maintain ignorance in order to perpetuate dominant and historical heteronormative norms (Curran, Chiarolli, & Pallotta-Chiarolli, 2009). This is easily seen in the discourse that children are "too young" to know about sexuality and gender expression/fluidity at the very same time that they are surrounded by normative heterosexuality in stories, movies, and cartoons that are unabashedly and unanimously viewed as "appropriate." Yet, Dryer (2019) argues that "the queer contours" of childhood allow for a broadened consideration of normal and, in fact, resist normative assessments of social and emotional growth (p. 6). We also draw upon the work of Gill-Peterson

(2018), Meiners (2016), and Sheldon (2016) – who in considering queer and trans-theories of childhood, posit that a queer lens allows for a perspective of childhood education that helps name and theorize the curiosity and imagination of childhood to protect the identities youth might claim in the future. The "tyranny of adult authority" in classrooms often overpowers the organic expressions of creativity and identity by children (Dryer, 2019, p. 6). By considering childhood as inherently unable to quantify or normalize, educators can empower children through their ability to play and create and form a world that does not reengage systems of oppression and, hopefully, interrupts the cycle of social reproduction. As Rob Simon and the Addressing Injustice Collective (2018) argue, teachers and advocates must be "working consciously to expect and prepare for individuals of multidimensional gender identities, sexualities, and family structures" (p. 143). It is heeding that call that we designed this study.

Methodological Approach

We framed our approach within a qualitative descriptive case study (Stake, 1995; Yin, 2002). Creswell (2014) noted qualitative research is an approach for "exploring and understanding the meaning individuals or groups ascribe to a social or human problem" (p. 4). In this case, the perceived reluctance of preservice elementary educators to include topics and issues of the LGBTQIA+ community as a component of diversity in the classroom, as well as their stated feelings of being ill-prepared to address the needs of LGBTQIA+ children and families in their future classroom. As teacher educators, this presented us with an opportunity to examine and address our own epistemological and ontological approaches. Hetherington (2013) concluded a methodology is the "link between ontology, epistemology, and theory informing the research, and the practice of conducting that research" (p. 72). The purpose of this case study then was to describe the phenomenon of the incorporation of LGBTQIA+ topics, issues, and materials into the elementary teacher preparation courses and to what extent that would challenge heteronormative and cisgender assumptions while better preparing them for teaching LGBTQIA+ children.

As described earlier in this chapter, data reported here resulted from a university-wide call to improve undergraduate writing. Given our concerns about the lack of emphasis on topics and issues impacting the LGBTQIA community within our teacher education program, we decided to focus our response to the writing initiative by asking two questions that would frame our approach:

(1) How might researching LGBTQIA+ topics to create multimodal writing projects contribute to combating heteronormativity and cisgender assumptions with preservice elementary teacher candidates?
(2) What (if any) shifts in preservice elementary education teacher candidates' perceptions or beliefs about working with children and/or families identifying as LGBTQIA+ occur after engaging in this project?

Our methodology allowed for the extrapolation of information by engaging participants in open dialogue in a familiar setting – in this case, college classrooms. As Creswell (2014) recommends, this approach allows us to interact with the participants on a human level and listen to and respond to their experiences while collecting rich and textual artifacts to describe both the process and experiences of the participants.

Pedagogical Approach

In designing our pedagogical approach to this research, we began with the awareness that when topics related to the LGBTQIA+ community are presented in teacher preparation at all, they typically receive far less attention than other areas of diversity (MacGillivray & Jennings, 2008; Sherwin & Jennings, 2006; Athanases & Larrabee, 2003). Moreover, once candidates leave the program and begin teaching in their classrooms, few opportunities for professional development are offered to teachers to gain knowledge about the LGBTQIA+ student experience (Payne & Smith, 2011). Thus, we were cognizant that while our efforts would not be nearly sufficient to adequately equip our preservice teachers with all of the knowledge they would need, it may well be one of the few opportunities they would have.

In a shift from prior approaches to these courses which focused largely on strategy instruction in the particular content area, we created assignments with a tripartite purpose: (1) they met the objectives of the respective courses, (2) they addressed the requirements of the grant we received to improve undergraduate interdisciplinary writing, and (3) they provided the teacher candidates with the opportunity to conduct meaningful research and produce multimodal text that addressed topics relevant to children and/or caregivers identifying as LGBTQIA+. We drew from Cappiello and Dawes (2014) definition of multigenre, multimodal text that includes an array of digital texts, including podcasts, videos, photographs, artistic works, and performances in addition to traditional print-based texts.

Within the courses, the instructors and students researched issues that impacted the LGBTQIA+ community. Students then selected an LGBTQIA+

topic or issue of concern they wanted to focus on to promote inclusivity. We selected the Queer Critical Media Literacies framework (Van Leent & Mills, 2018) to assist them in their research as it speaks to pedagogical and learning experiences across our courses. According to Van Leent and Mills (2018), this framework "synthesizes key LGBTQIA+ research sources to distill and refine a set of pedagogical approaches to . . . critique heteronormative assumptions of texts . . . and multimodal and digital practices" (Van Leent & Mills, 2018, p. 403).

Students then identified relevant knowledge and credible sources related to this topic. Each student had the opportunity to choose a topic, which digital tool(s) to use, and the artifact's final form. This approach allowed for each instructor to address the writing standards required in the grant and our focus on LGBTQIA+ issues in complementary but course-specific ways. For example, in the English Language Arts Methods course, a student opted to use a free digital storytelling tool to write a story for young students about her sibling's coming out as transgender using the allegory of a butterfly. In the Instructional Technology course, students created infographics about LGBTQIA+ issues, such as gender-neutral bathrooms and pronoun usage.

In addition to the resources, we were able to provide faculty such as exemplar picture books and websites; we also invited community members from the local LGBT Outreach, student members from the campus GSA, as well as Judith's (author) transgender teenaged son, Camden, to come in and talk with our candidates about their experiences. It should be noted, however, that Camden only participated in the second semester as those students seemed especially resistant to accepting trans students. Upon hearing about this, Camden volunteered to come into the class to help the candidates see that "he was just a regular kid."

Data Sources and Collection

Data for this research include the participating students' written and digital artifacts, surveys of attitudes and dispositions about the LGBTQIA+ community, instructor lesson plans, and transcripts from focus groups with participating students collected within the two teacher education courses over the two-semester period. Participants were duly consented and had the option to not participate in the study. However, all students were asked to complete the assignments as part of the regular classwork. For students who were gravely disturbed by the content of the assignment, an alternative topic related to diversity was made available in keeping with IRB requirements.

Analysis of these data utilized initial in vivo coding (Saldaña, 2016) drawing from the participants' own words and writing. The research team then utilized collaborative coding (Smagorinsky, 2008), to review, discuss the codes emerging from each class set of data together. Smagorinsky asserts, "we reach agreement on each code through collaborative discussion rather than independent corroboration" (p. 401). Codes were then organized by themes that emerged as the result of deep engagement with the data as well as from in-depth conversations to their meaning. Thematic analysis yielded a continuum framework to explain the range of reactions and texts produced by the teacher candidates that we denoted as "Dimensions of Allyship."

Dimensions of Allyship Framework

We created our analytic framework drawing from a model that describes three dimensions of citizenship: personally responsible, participatory, and justice oriented (Westheimer, 2015; Westheimer & Kahne, 2004). These researchers categorize levels of citizenship across three dimensions. The personally responsible citizen uses individual efforts to contribute to the society. For example, she might contribute used books to a book drive at a local school or outreach. At a somewhat higher level of involvement, the participatory citizen might recognize the needs of a school or community group and engage in organizing the book drive. Finally, the third level involves proactive engagement, which mirrors some of the tenets of critical literacy/pedagogy such as challenging unjust societal structures and listening for the voices of the silenced. The justice-oriented citizen seeks to advocate and act for a systemic change in the conditions that perpetuate issues of access and inequity and illiteracy in historically resilient, yet institutionally underserved populations (Echo-Hawk, 2019).

In seeing parallels between citizenship and allyship, we shifted the focus described previously to engagement with and advocacy for, LGBTQIA+ students, parents, and the issues facing the community *writ large* to create this model of ally-citizenship. Although Westheimer and Kahne do not describe these dimensions as necessarily hierarchical, we position our dimensions along a continuum ranging from disengaged/apathetic to ally/advocate (see Figure 4.1.)

As illustrated previously, the dimensions we describe create a continuum from Disengaged through ally and reflect codes that we believed fell within these larger themes. This is not to imply, however, that these dimensions or stages are static or that forward movement or even regression is not possible. Rather the continuum and the stages or dimensions are meant to function as a frame of reference for what we believe is the ever-developing stance of allyship.

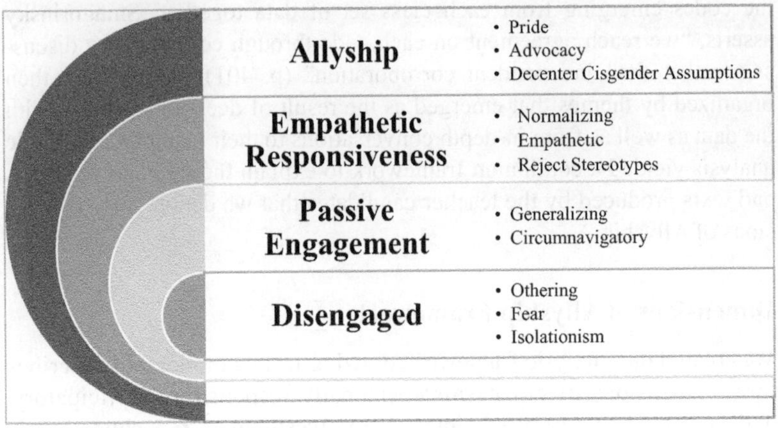

Figure 4.1 Dimensions of Allyship

Disengaged

This theme arose from the analytic codes in the data that reflected notions of othering, fear, and isolationism –both in the relevance of the topic and in their role as teachers addressing it. While not blatantly homo/transphobic, and certainly insisting that they were not, students whose work and discussions feel within this dimension expressed a profound discomfort with addressing LGBTQIA+ issues or discrimination in the classroom, with the most extreme reaction condemning of the "lifestyle" due to religious beliefs. While certainly a smaller percentage of the class, a few students were, as Ryan and Hermann-Wilmarth (2018) found, "entirely unwilling to consider LGBTQ-inclusive education under any circumstance" (p. 2).

The majority of these students, however, generally espoused the belief that students, and especially elementary-aged children, were indeed "too young and innocent" to be exposed to these topics, even when presented as part of an inclusionary curriculum or approach to school climate. They exemplified attitudes and beliefs described by Pallotta-Chiarolli (1999) as a characteristic of challenging (or not) "safe" and "unsafe" prejudices. "Safe-to-challenge" prejudices include racism, ethnocentrism, and (cisgender) sexism. While "unsafe-to-challenge" and "inappropriate-to-challenge" prejudices include homophobia, transphobia, and heterosexism. As evidenced in her study with practicing educators and again two decades later in ours, we regrettably report that for some, these prejudices are still being denied, silenced, and ignored even as teachers espouse support for an "inclusive curriculum" and "safe schools" (Pallotta-Chiarolli, 1999, p. 191). Perhaps unsurprisingly, the artifacts produced by these students as well as their reluctant engagement with the topic in-class discussion and focus groups reflected the "safe" versus "unsafe" binary and situated our project firmly in the "unsafe" category.

Passive Engagement

While some students created projects that demonstrated reflective thinking as their understanding of their topic shifted and became more expansive, we found that a significant percentage of students who reported that they were accepting of LGBTQIA+ children or families in a survey, still created texts that reflected generalized themes that avoided direct mention of LGBTQIA+ experiences. One of the hallmarks of this stage was a desire to circumnavigate topics and/or issues relevant to the LGBTQIA+ community under a general umbrella of anti-bullying or acceptance of reversed stereotypical gender roles, that is, girls playing football or men cooking dinner.) While children's books with themes of anti-bullying and/or acceptance of non-traditional gender roles are certainly of value, the students who created these texts visibly and vocally shied away from taking a direct approach to the topics they researched. Instead, their work and the attitudes behind them reflected an approach rooted in binary categories. There are the bullies and the bullied. There are the accepted and the shunned. There are boys and there are girls – but all should be treated equally.

However, our lived realities, and certainly of LGBTQIA+ youth, are almost always more complicated than the broad strokes of binary categories suggest. Teacher candidates represented in this stage of the framework were particularly resistant to moving beyond the binary and experienced difficulty in conceiving the intersectionality of experiences and identities outside of what Judith Butler termed the heterosexual matrix (Butler, 2006). While challenged in more recent research as situated within colonial and imperial histories (Moreira, 2020; Patil, 2018), the heterosexual matrix describes a tripartite system of gender/sex assigned at birth/sexuality which is seen as an interconnected set of binaries that influence our interpretations and beliefs about how (cisgender) men and women are to look, behave, and be attracted to. Functioning within this matrix, the teacher candidates in this stage felt that disrupting traditional or stereotypical gender roles was analogous to allyship and advocacy for LGBTQIA+ children and/or families.

Empathetic Responsiveness

Those teacher candidates falling within this stage of the framework may have been initially reticent when we first broached the project in class; however, they rapidly demonstrated a sense of empathy that propelled their conversations, reflections, and book projects. The characteristics of this stage included a desire to normalize a myriad of identities, including LGBTQIA+ while also rejecting both "traditional" gender roles/identities and more hurtful negative stereotypes. In this stage, we also observed a greater degree of responsiveness to individual differences – indeed, most students were quick to point out that it is the differences among us that make everyone special. Unlike the students in the passive disengagement stage, they were able to see past and through the heterosexual matrix and commented on how it had influenced their thoughts and beliefs in the past.

However, while the defining characteristic of the members of this stage was an overarching desire to reject stereotypes, interestingly no examples of negative stereotypes or their perilous consequences were offered. Instead, the books created by this group depicted acceptance but stopped short of advocacy. While this dichotomy of acceptance versus advocacy might seem an exercise in semantics, for the purposes of this research, we differentiate between them due to what we saw as degrees of engagement. For example, while teacher candidates in this stage demonstrated a whole-hearted and vocal acceptance of children and/or families identifying as LGBTQIA+ and their books focused on topics such as using claimed pronouns and names, the action stopped there. In other words, the candidates demonstrated personal acceptance but did not seem to want to publicly advocate or take action on a systemic level. Like the participatory citizen described by Westheimer and Kahne (2004), who organizes food or clothing drives but does not interrogate the systemic causes of food insecurity and poverty, members of this stage saw it as a personal moral imperative to promote acceptance but did not explore why it was needed in the first place.

Allyship

This culminating, yet evolving, stage of the Dimensions of Allyship framework denoted action as imperative to advocacy. In contrast to the preceding stage of empathetic responsiveness which featured personal acceptance, in this stage, the teacher candidates and the artifacts they created called for the recognition that systemic and historic injustices undergirding current discrimination. Moreover, the members of this group wanted to go beyond accepting claimed names and pronouns to robustly decentering cisgender assumptions and privilege. Indeed, at this stage, teacher candidates were especially vocal about the need to create and advocate for, inclusive environments for all children and families identifying as LGBTQIA+, but especially for those children who are transgender and/or gender fluid.

In a 180-degree shift from their disengaged or even passively engaged counterparts, some common characteristics of this group included a desire to learn more about issues impacting the LGBTQIA+ community, a willingness to speak up and out to challenge the binary of "safe" and "unsafe" to question discrimination as described by Pallotta-Chiarolli (1999). These students also spoke about the need for representation of diverse gender expression in the classroom and in the need for a queered curriculum (Blackburn & Pascoe, 2015) that directly faces the "difficult knowledge" (Britzman, 1998) of the historic educational exclusion of LGBTQIA+ youth. While this study did not follow the teacher candidates into their own classrooms to see if the desire to engage in public allyship came to fruition, we are hopeful that the recognition they highlighted of the importance of teachers – especially elementary teachers – to be advocates remains in their current practice.

While these dimensions and stages are not meant to be inclusive of every experience, belief, or attitude, and while there is certainly overlap in and between the stages, the framework was helpful for us as both teacher educators and researchers to begin to conceptualize what we were seeing with our elementary teacher candidates. We also seek to avoid an oversimplification of the process and progress from disengaged to allyship. Many, if not all our students, even those whose discussions and artifacts reflected what we termed "allyship" still struggled or even experienced discomfort in grappling with how to create an inclusive classroom for LGBTQIA+ children and families, while still maintaining the often-tenuous balance between personal beliefs and what parents, administrators, and the general public might see as "appropriate" for children.

Yet, this discomfort and struggle, in itself a crisis of recognizing and grappling with their heterosexual privilege and the benefits enjoyed through systemic heteronormativity, is not one teacher educators should attempt to shield their students from or be caught off guard by. Yet, as Shoshana Felman (1995) suggests, "Educators should expect students to enter crisis." In fact, she argues that "teaching in itself, teaching as such, takes place precisely only through crisis" (p. 7). In the following chapters, we invite you to join us as we navigated with our students in a space that was intended to facilitate teacher candidates' journey through that crisis to challenge the oppression historically experienced by LGBTQIA+ children and their families in education. We also reflect on our process and progress as we sought to provide guidance about topics, issues, and research that we were largely learning along with our students. We especially invite you as the reader, to reflect on your own experiences (or not) related to the inclusion of LGBTQIA+ topics, in your field of research or your institutions' approaches to diversity and inclusion.

References

Aronson, B., & Laughter, J. (2020). The theory and practice of culturally relevant education: expanding the conversation to include gender and sexuality equity. *Gender and Education*, *32*(2), 262–279.

Athansases, S., & Larrabee, T. (2003). Toward a consistent stance in teaching for equity: Learning to advocate for lesbian and gay-identified youth. *Teaching and Teacher Education*, *19*(2), 237–261.

Blackburn, M. V., & Clark, C. T. (2011). Analyzing talk in a long-term literature discussion group: Ways of operating within LGBT-inclusive and queer discourses. *Reading Research Quarterly*, *46*(3), 222–248.

Blackburn, M. V., & Pascoe, C. J. (2015). K – 12 students in schools. In G. Wimberly (Ed.), *LGBTQ issues in education: Advancing a research agenda* (pp. 89–104). Washington, DC: American Educational Research Association.

Britzman, D. P. (1998). *Lost subjects, contested objects: Toward a psychoanalytic inquiry of learning*. New York: State University of New York Press.

Brockenbrough, E. (2015). Queer of color agency in educational contexts: Analytic frameworks from a queer of color critique. *Educational Studies*, *51*(1), 28–44.

Bryson, M., & De Castell, S. (1993). Queer pedagogy: Praxis makes im/perfect. *Canadian Journal of Education/Revue canadienne de l'éducation*, 285–305.

Butler, J. (2006). *Gender trouble: Feminism and the subversion of identity*. New York: Routledge (First published in 1990).

Cappiello, M., & Dawes, E. (2014). *Teaching with text sets*. Shell Education. Kindle Edition.

Carspecken, P. F. (1996). *Critical ethnography in educational research*. New York: Routledge.

Creswell, J. W. (2014). *Qualitative, quantitative and mixed methods approaches*. Sage.

Curran, G., Chiarolli, S., & Pallotta-Chiarolli, M. (2009). 'The C Words': clitorises, childhood and challenging compulsory heterosexuality discourses with pre-service primary teachers. *Sex Education*, *9*(2), 155–168.

Dryer, H. (2019). *The Queer Aesthetics of Childhood: Asymmetries of Innocence and the Cultural Politics of Child Development*. Rutgers University Press.

Echo-Hawk, A. (2019, September 7). Twitter. https://twitter.com/echohawkd3/status/1170371608894046208

Enciso, P. (2007). Reframing history in sociocultural theories: Toward an expansive vision. In C. Lewis, P. Enciso, & E. Moje (Eds.), *Reframing sociocultural research on literacy: Identity, agency, and power* (pp. 49–74). Mahwah, NJ: Erlbaum.

Felman, S. (1995). Education and crisis, or the vicissitudes of teaching. *Trauma: Explorations in Memory*, *13*.

Gill-Peterson, J. (2018). *Histories of the Transgender Child.* Minneapolis: University of Minnesota Press.

Hetherington, L. (2013). Complexity Thinking and Methodology: The Potential of "Complex Case Study" for Educational Research. *Complicity: An International Journal of Complexity and Education, 10*, 71–85.

Jagose, A. (1996). *Queer theory: An introduction.* NYU Press.

Janks, H. (2017). Critical literacy and the social justice project of education. *English Teaching: Practice & Critique, 16*(2), 132–144.

Keenan, D. (2012). Marriage and the Homosexual Body: It's About Race. *Journal of homosexuality, 59*(9), 1230–1258.

Ladson-Billings, G. (2006). Yes, but how do we do it? Practicing culturally relevant pedagogy. In J. Landsman & C.W. Lewis (Eds.), *White teachers/diverse classrooms: A guide to building inclusive schools, promoting high expectations, and eliminating racism* (pp. 29–42). Sterling, VA: Stylus.

La Salle, T. P., Wang, C., Wu, C., & Rocha Neves, J. (2020). Racial mismatch among minoritized students and white teachers: Implications and recommendations for moving forward. *Journal of Educational and Psychological Consultation, 30*(3), 314–343.

Macgillivray, I., & Jennings, T. (2008). A content analysis exploring lesbian, gay, bisexual, and transgender topics in foundations of education textbooks. *Journal of Teacher Education, 59*(2), 170–188.

McEntarfer, H. K. (2016). *Navigating gender and sexuality in the classroom: Narrative insights from students and educators*. New York: Routledge.

Meiners, E. (2006). *For the Children? Protecting Innocence in a Carceral State.* Minneapolis: Minnesota University Press.

Miller, S. (2015). A Queer Literacy Framework Promoting (A) Gender and (A) Sexuality Self-Determination and Justice. *English Journal, 104*(5), 37–44.

Moreira, L. (2020). Doing intimate citizenship: Resisting the heterosexual matrix across and beyond intimacy. *Sexuality & Culture, 24*(6), 1875–1892.

Morrell, E. (2008). *Critical literacy and urban youth: Pedagogies of access, dissent, and liberation.* New York: Routledge.

Pallotta-Chiarolli, M. (1999). Diary entries from the "Teachers' Professional Development Playground", *Journal of Homosexuality, 36*(3–4), 183–205. DOI: 10.1300/J082v36n03_12

Patil, V. (2018). The heterosexual matrix as imperial effect. *Sociological Theory, 36*(1), 1–26.

Payne, E., & Smith, M. (2011). The reduction of stigma in schools: A new professional development model for empowering educators to support LGBTQ students. *Journal of LGBTQ Youth, 8(2)*, 174–200.

Ryan, C. L., & Hermann-Wilmarth, J. M. (2018). *Reading the rainbow: LGBTQ-inclusive literacy instruction in the elementary classroom.* Teachers College Press.

Saldaña, J. (2016). Goodall's verbal exchange coding: An overview and example. *Qualitative Inquiry, 22*(1), 36–39.

Sherwin, G., & Jennings, T. (2006). Feared, forgotten, or forbidden: Sexual orientation topics in secondary teacher preparation programs in the USA. *Teaching Education, 17*(3), 207–223.

Sheldon, R. (2016). *The Child to Come: Life after the Human Catastrophe*. Minnesota University Press.

Simon, R., Walkland, T., Gallagher, B., Evis, S., & Baer, P. (2018). Breaking Gender Expectations: Adolescents' Critical Rewriting of a Trans Young Adult Novel. In *Literacies, Sexualities, and Gender* (pp. 141–154). Routledge.

Sleeter, C. E. (2001). Preparing teachers for culturally diverse schools: Research and the overwhelming presence of whiteness. *Journal of Teacher Education, 52*(2), 94–106. https://doi.org/10.1177/0022487101052002002

Smagorinsky, P. (2008). The method section as conceptual epicenter in constructing social science research reports. *Written communication, 25*(3), 389–411.

Somerville, S. B. (2000). *Queering the Color Line: Race and the Invention of Homosexuality in American Culture*. Duke University Press.

Stake, R. W. (1995). *The art of case study research*. Thousand Oaks, CA: Sage.

Tolbert, J. B. (2019). Prisms of Whiteness: A critical analysis of the multicultural competence of pre-service teachers. *International Journal of Learning, Teaching and Educational Research, 18*(4), 141–157.

Thomas-Reid, M. (2018). *Queer Pedagogy*. [online] Available at https://oxfordre.com

Thomas, E. E., Bean-Folkes, J., & Coleman, J. J. (2020). Restorying critical literacies. In Moje, E. B., Afflerbach, P. P., Enciso, P., & Lesaux, N. K. (Eds.) *Handbook of Reading Research*, Volume V. New York: Routledge.

Van Leent, L., & Mills, K. (2018). A queer critical media literacies framework in a digital age. *Journal of Adolescent & Adult Literacy, 61*(4), 401–411.

Westheimer, J. (2015). *What kind of citizen: Educating our children for the common good*. New York: Teachers College Press.

Westheimer, J., & Kahne, J. (2004). What kind of citizen? The politics of educating for democracy. *American Educational Research Journal, 41*(2), 237–269.

Yin, R. K. (2002). *Case study research: Design and methods*. Thousand Oaks, CA: SAGE Publications.

Zacko-Smith, J. D., & Smith, G. P. (2010). Recognizing and Utilizing Queer Pedagogy: A Call for Teacher Education to Reconsider the Knowledge Base on Sexual Orientation for Teacher Education Programs. *Multicultural Education, 18*(1), 2–9.

5 The Dimensions of Allyship Framework

Stages and Progressions

In this chapter, we share the findings from our study that resulted in the thematic development of the Dimensions of Allyship framework (see Figure 5.1). Across all the stages, our findings suggest that a queered pedagogy in elementary teacher education programs is needed to proactively combat heteronormativity in schools. In general, findings indicate that teacher candidates experienced shifts in their acceptance of, knowledge about, and understanding of LGBTQIA+ topics and issues during the study. For example, in presurvey/postsurvey data, while over 80% of students indicated that they were openly accepting of gay, lesbian, and bisexual people in initial survey data, only 59% felt the same way for transgender individuals. By the end of the study, however, nearly 79% of students indicated they were openly accepting of trans individuals. While encouraging to some degree, 21% of teacher candidates remained either "uncomfortable" or "very uncomfortable" with the prospect of having a child who identified as transgender in their classrooms. Likewise, in answer to the question, "As a future teacher, how comfortable would you be discussing, planning activities or advocating for LGBTQIA+ issues and students with other teachers" there was only a 16% increase in students responding that they would be either "extremely comfortable" or "moderately comfortable" doing so in their future classrooms.

While survey findings indicated shifts in perception and perspectives about LGBTQIA+ individuals, we did not find them entirely reflected in the artifacts the candidates produced, or in their focus group conversations and final written reflections. Although some students created projects that demonstrated reflective thinking as their understanding of their topic shifted and became more expansive, we found that a significant percentage of students who reported accepting LGBTQIA+ children or families in a survey still created texts that reflected apathetic or disengaged themes. We found this dichotomy to be both interesting and challenging as we worked with students to create multimodal texts that would be inclusive and act as

DOI: 10.4324/9781003110934-5

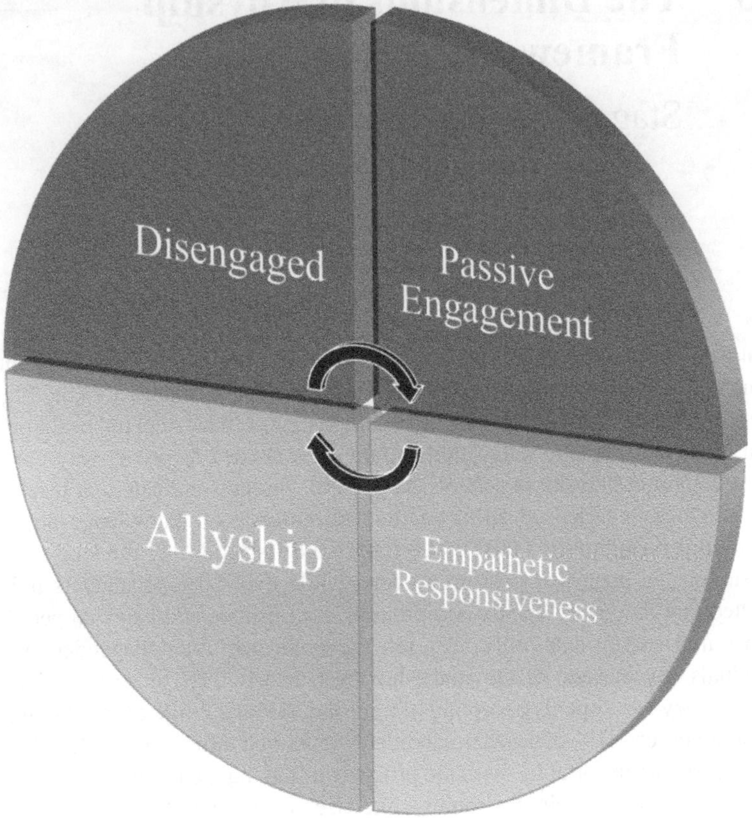

Figure 5.1 Dimensions of Allyship Framework With Early Stages Emphasized

a catalyst for a meaningful dialogic exchange (Bahktin, 1981) on a subject that genuinely worried many of them.

We turn now to the four stages, namely: disengaged, passive engagement, empathetic responsiveness, and allyship. We next provide exemplars to illustrate the range of responses and artifacts across these four stages and discuss the progression of some students and the static response of others.

Disengaged

Data evidenced that some of our participants fell under the category of disengaged for a variety of reasons including reflecting fear (either of the topic or reaction to it), isolationism, and notions of othering. Mirroring the participants in Payne and Smith's (2011) study, our student reactions to thinking about having a transgender student in their future classroom included "freak out," "panic," "crisis," "fear," and "unprepared" (pp. 404–405). That was quite evident in one teacher candidates' comments during our final focus group:

> I am still . . . scared. I'm not sure yet if I put it in my teaching, how to properly present it. Will the kids understand what I'm trying to get across? And also another thing is parents. Sometimes parents are not 100% all there yet as of now. A lot of parents are comfortable with talking about certain things like that, but a lot of parents are old school, and if I end up bringing it into my classroom, and the child goes back home and asks their parents, and their parents go, "Well, wait a minute, I didn't send you so school to learn about that." So, it's just making sure that I don't cross that line.

Although these candidates willingly participated in the study, creating the required artifacts and participating in focus groups, they showed discomfort ranging from mild to significant, when addressing topics related to the LGBTQIA+ community in the classroom. Some admitted to being unwilling to even think about approaching the subject with students, while others felt like to indicate acceptance was "immoral" and contrary to their personal beliefs. Indeed, in the focus groups, one teacher candidate bluntly stated:

> It has been uncomfortable. [My parents and friends] just look at me like, you're doing it? This doesn't mess with your morals or what you believe in? I'm like at this point you gotta put that to the side, get the grade and keep moving.

This theme of discomfort was quite prevalent with several candidates and tended to correspond with a "teacher pleasing" approach of just wanting to be done with the methods courses and this project and put it behind them. Another way discomfort manifested was more in response to external, rather than internal factors. For these students, it wasn't as much about being personally disengaged or uncomfortable, their discomfort lay in the projected responses of other teachers, administrators, and most of all, the parents of their future students. This was exemplified by another who said, "I'm uncomfortable. I'm just not comfortable . . . too comfortable with how to approach it with my actual students. How do I introduce this without making others uncomfortable?" This feeling or fear of negative consequences was echoed by other participants who felt like students at the elementary level were too young or innocent to deal with these topics or who did not, for lack of better terms, want to deal with the parents of these students who may not agree with the topic being addressed. The trope of "childhood" as an innocent space in need of heteronormative protection against queer threat (Robinson, 2013) was clearly operationalized for these teacher candidates.

Similarly, other students wondered aloud about how creating an LGBTQIA+ inclusive classroom might oppose "traditional" values and beliefs and what it means to be a "safe" space for students, especially in the conservative Bible Belt of the United States. This too was indicative of what Robinson and Davies (2018) refer to as the "moral panic" of right-wing actors whose views have dominated American education – especially elementary education for decades. This was especially apparent in the ways that discrimination against sexual orientation and/or gender identification was reified to "sexuality" as a physical act rather than as identity. The irony that heterosexuality and cisgender identities, even when toxic or misogynistic is well represented in every classroom library from the earliest of grades, did not seem to be recognized by many teacher candidates (Brody, 2020; Cassidy & Kehler, 2018; Marshall, 2004). Common too, in this stage in the Dimensions of Allyship framework, was a comparison to race and culture as safe to include in conversations about diversity in classrooms (Pallotta-Chiarolli, 1999), whereas discussions related to LGBTQIA+ discrimination were not. One example of this from a student reflection reads:

> While race and the issues that come along with race have always been taught in the classroom, sexuality has not. This will be something new in the classroom and I think that is where my discomfort comes from. I think with time the schools and teachers will become more comfortable teaching this subject, but as of now, I would not want to go [in the classroom] and teach on this topic.

Another teacher candidate was worried about how her beliefs would transfer to the children. She engages in a bit of soul-searching and contemplated how to balance her personal beliefs about LGBTQIA+ individuals without imposing them on her students. As a self-described Evangelical Christian, she believed that homosexuality was a sin and that marriage was the purview of cisgender, straight men and women. As we will see in subsequent chapters, this is juxtaposed with teacher candidates who were personally supportive of LGBTQIA+ people and empathetic to the issues they face but still didn't want to influence their future students. One student spoke about this internal struggle in our final focus group:

> I also feel like with you saying that that's important because you've got to make [students] understand that people have the right to have those

> beliefs, but you also have to tell them, you don't have to believe what I believe or what they believe, you have to believe what you . . . so I appreciate you bringing that up because it's hard for a person to understand. You have to stay neutral, but you also have to be true to what you believe.

Other teacher candidates expressed a desire to just learn teaching methods without any conversations that they saw as liberal political correctness, while some wished, "we just didn't have to talk about this." While in a classroom discussion another student flatly stated, "I'll never discriminate, but I can't condone this either. It is against my beliefs." While she did face some backlash from her peers for this position, as critical educators, we aimed to make space for all voices.

Students who were apathetic or even diametrically opposed to the inclusion of LGBTQIA+ topics, materials, or discussion in primary classrooms were encouraged to participate in dialogic exchange and share their views and the conflicts they were experiencing. We saw this as an opportunity to acknowledge their position and yet also draw parallels between civil and human rights that cannot be subject to individual viewpoints or religious beliefs. We were also able to discuss recent scholarship calling for religious schools to recognize that the discrimination directed at LGBTQIA+ youth is antithetical to Christian ethics of justice (Joldersma, 2016). Moreover, for students who were tempted to ridicule or chastise those who were disengaged, there was an opportunity to discuss anti-religious views as a bias within itself (McEntarfer, 2016).

While less resistant to the research and multimodal book creation assignment, other students who we saw as reflecting disengaged or apathetic stances created texts that vaguely and opaquely addressed LGBTQIA+ issues under the guise of being generally tolerant of various individual differences. This was frequently portrayed as a character who did not quite fit in or was excluded for quirky personality traits or clothing choices. For example, one student created a book entitled, *Harper Lester and her Boyish Ways*. In this book, a young girl named Harper dresses in what other characters in the story perceive as "boys' clothes" and engages in activities that may be considered traditionally male. However, while we acknowledge that the student was making an honest attempt to be accepting of nonbinary individuals, everything in the book was presented as a "choice" Harper was making, rather than an innate part of her identity.

While we admit to harboring concerns about the students who appeared disengaged once they reach classrooms of their own, they were not entirely without some forward movement and positive shifts in perceptions. It would be inaccurate to say otherwise and not helpful to decry their beliefs and positionality. Rather, we see it as an opportunity to continue to work

Figure 5.2 Harper Lester and Her Boyish Ways – Example of Disengaged Text

with students at this stage of progression, and as a rationale to ensuring that the inclusion of LGBTQIA+ topics, history, and issues be woven throughout the elementary teacher education program.

Passive Engagement

By contrast, the students who reflected passive engagement tended to circumnavigate the issues faced by the LGBTQIA+ community by comparing their experiences to those who are discriminated against because of race or culture but in a manner analogous to the problematic "colorblind" approach. We described this as circumnavigating the issues at hand, rather than directly addressing them. In our use here, students who were "circumnavigating" acknowledged that people need support and that we should all accept our differences; however, LGBTQIA+ difference was seen as one of many idiosyncratic permutations or group membership.

These students' multimodal books featured characters defying gender stereotypes in action and dress, or used comparisons to race and culture, or sometimes both. For example, one student created a picture book about a young African American girl named Mia, who wanted to play football. Although her friends ridiculed her, Mia's parents offer encouragement and support. Another student used the analogy of a box of crayons to illustrate her view that all colors are important and everyone has a role to play in creating the "big picture." A third book portrayed a female cat that liked to wear a blue ribbon instead of a pink one. Her friend who is a dog initially mocks her. However, by the end of the story, he compliments her on her choice. While these books and others reflected in this stage generally had uplifting and inclusive messages, there remains the implication that these are personal choices to be supported, rather than innate and integral embodiments of identity.

In classroom discussions and in the focus groups, students who were in this stage would say things like, "I can't understand why people get upset – it's not that big a deal" in describing others' intolerance. However, another student, clearly frustrated, asked our LGBTQIA+ consultant, "Can't we just teach the idea of acceptance, without breaking it down into all this [LGBTQIA+] stuff?" Her question was honest, yet it belied the undercurrent of positioning that defined this group: It is enough to be accepting of all people; we don't really need to differentiate between groups. For example, one student reflected:

> As a future teacher, I understand that I have to train myself not to associate things with gender. This can really limit the students' dreams and beliefs. Overall, I learned that these concepts don't have to be awkward or turned into a big deal. These are concepts that should be presented and acknowledged in a positive way – just like everything else.

Another teacher candidate generalized the need to include resources and conversations related to sexualities and gender in the classroom to include experiences they had moving to many different places with the US military. The student said,

> "I feel like that's how I've grown up throughout my life, having multiple varieties of culture and stuff and I feel grateful for that. So, I feel like it's a good experience for me as a military brat, so I would like for kids to have that same experience."

Many of these candidates simply believed that being a member of the LGBTQIA+ community was not unlike being a member of any other institutionally and/or colonially oppressed race or culture. These candidates' artifacts and comments centered on tolerance and acceptance of different people or even nonbinary self-expression; however, it was always measured against traditional gender roles embedded in straight, cisgender identities. While making generalizations across historically resilient, but systemically marginalized groups was a hallmark of this stage, one of the more

When I'm sad, unsure of who I am
and don't know what to do...I
reach into my crayon box, they
have always seen me through.

Figure 5.3 My Crayon Box – Example of a Passively Engaged Text

Source: Image courtesy of Sharon McCutcheon from Pexels

problematic generalizations made equated accepting LGBTQIA+ students as analogous to being "color-blind" in regard to treating children of different races, religions, and cultures the same.

The color-blind trope has historically provided White teachers with "powerful explanations – which ultimately become justifications – for contemporary racial inequality that exculpates them from any responsibility for the status of people of color" (Bonilla-Silva, 2013, p. 2). So too, does the parallel stance of what we have coined as "rainbow-blindness" apply to LGBTQIA+ individuals. Although we do not contend that the historic oppression experienced by various groups are equivalent, we do see parallels in the belief systems operationalized here, including the same sort of language patterns: "I do not see X (a Black child, gay child, etc.), I only see a child," etc. However, much like with race, this blindness toward gender and/or sexuality acts as a form of violent erasure that ensures inequality without culpability for the perpetrator. Of all the stages in our framework, this group was perhaps the most challenging, as their positioning was the most resistant to engaging in allyship, as they believed tolerance alone was the goal as evidenced in reflections such as this:

> I had never really thought that LGBTQ+ inclusivity would ever have to be anything I'd address in my 1st-grade classroom. Alas, the more and more I was researching, I realized it wasn't necessarily about LGBTQ+ specifically that would be addressed with my 6-year-olds,

> rather accepting one another for who they are. Like with race – I don't see it. All children are the same. Therefore, I wrote my children's book with that in mind – creating a welcoming and inclusive classroom for all "rockstar classmates" who may look different from others, or like different things than what society deems "correct."

Stances like this were very difficult to challenge, because to the teacher candidate, they were being fair and seeing everyone as equal. As other researchers have found, the colorblind approach is "deemed so well-intentioned that it is hard to fight against" (Choi, 2008, p. 53). Whereas the students who were more disengaged were often so due to religious convictions or fear of the reactions of other stakeholders, they were somewhat aware that those stances may have a negative impact on the children they will teach.

In the passively engaged dimension, however, the neoliberal beliefs evidenced in a colorblind approach (Perez & Salter, 2019) reinforce straight/cisgender hegemony in schools and out. Instead of interrogating the false "everyone is equal" liberal meritocracy, these future teachers seemed willing to ignore the lived experiences of the LGBTQIA+ community, and instead white-washed the rainbow in their efforts to create inclusive classrooms. Although we were somewhat frustrated with the almost immoveable positioning of our students in this stage of the Allyship framework, we are very cognizant that they are products of neoliberal thought that dominates K-12 and higher education. Much like with their disengaged counterparts, these students underscore the need for teacher education programs to engage in LGBQIA+ inclusive pedagogy and curriculum if we are to expect our future teachers to do so as well.

We turn now to discuss the last two stages of our Dimensions of Allyship framework: empathic responsiveness and allyship (see Figure 5.4). These stages distinguish themselves from the initial stages of disengaged and passive engagement because of the marked departure from feelings of irrelevance and generalizations to those of recognition and advocacy. Those teacher candidates represented in this stage of the framework see beyond binaries and acknowledge the individual colors and shading of and across the metaphorical rainbow.

Speaking broadly, those teacher candidates designated as empathic progressed from possible feelings of resistance and/or hesitation to empathic and benevolent feelings, as well as the personal acceptance of LGBTQIA+ children and families. However, the stage of empathetic responsiveness is markedly different from the full actualization of allyship because of a lack of criticality of systemic level discrimination and committed advocacy. As we have alluded to previously, the difference in empathic responsiveness and allyship is more than semantic. Instead, it is the difference between

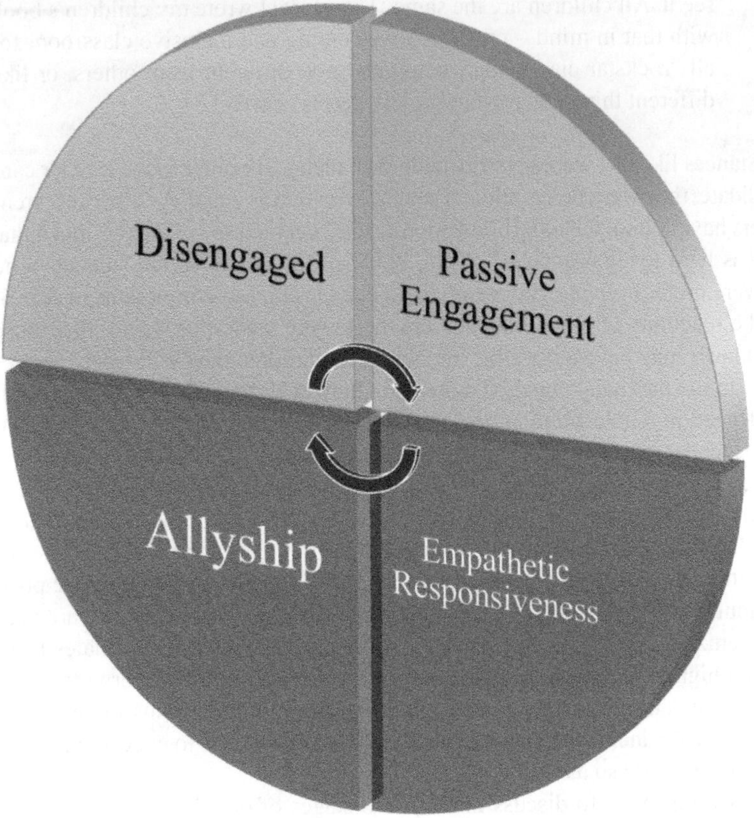

Figure 5.4 Dimensions of Allyship Framework With Late Stages Emphasized

recognizing equity and promoting equity. It is in this actionable final stage in which teacher candidates directly address historic, systemic, and engrained discrimination. Beyond feelings of empathy, allyship is the decentering of harmful heterogenous dichotomies, rather than just the avoidance of such; it is the disruption of stereotypes, rather than the absence of such; and finally, it is the creation of space that is not only welcoming but also celebratory of the spectrum of gender identity and expression, rather than simple platitudes about the importance of such.

The actualization of allyship, while evolving, is essential in, by, and for teachers – especially elementary teachers – as classrooms seek not only to reflect curricular and pedagogical practices that foster equity and inclusiveness but also to generate and instill allyship and advocacy in all students, thus changing the environment. As Kendi (2019) discusses in his framework for antiracism, the idea of not being racist is distinct from the act of being antiracist. The active process of building a truly antiracist society, according to Kendi, has less to do with doing no harm and everything to do with generating advocacy for policies, environments, sentiments, perspectives, and tolerance for equity: "the opposite of 'racist' isn't 'not racist; it is 'antiracist'" (Kendi, 2019, p. 2). Ours is a similar perspective with regard to embracing LGBTQIA+ students, families, and experiences, especially in classrooms and most especially by teachers. The opposite of a discriminatory and exclusionary classroom is not one that disabuses itself of these notions. Instead, it seeks to create movers and shakers of change that directly combat and disassemble discrimination.

Thus, in differentiating the degrees of engagement that distinguish the final two stages of the Dimensions of Allyship framework by way of facilitating and encouraging teachers, teacher candidates, and teacher educators to distinguish between developing more positive beliefs and perspectives toward LGBTQIA+ children and families toward consciously and proactively engage in advocacy.

Empathetic Responsiveness

That data which evidenced empathetic responsiveness from teacher candidates were accompanied by reflections of early resistance and hesitation, implying a characteristic of marked growth and significant growth at that. One teacher candidate commented, "I had no idea how important it would be to discuss things like LGBTQ+ [sic] inclusivity in my [future] 1st-grade classroom. I actually panicked." This same teacher candidate continued by stating that the realization of the importance of the LGBTQIA+ curriculum in their future classroom was really a poignant reminder about inclusivity: "The more and more I researched, I realized that it isn't necessarily about LGBTQ+ [sic] specifically that would be addressed with my 6-year-olds, rather accepting another for who they are regardless of gender." While this evidence is beyond the second stage of the dimensions of allyship framework, this teacher candidate's reflections indicate avoiding the promotion of diversity and individual recognition in favor of the sweeping notion of appreciating differences. While this is progress, it is firmly situated in the stage that precedes – rather than actualizes – action and allyship. Thus, this teacher candidate is designed as empathic.

A similar reflection found that while the topic of LGBTQIA+ in elementary classrooms was not only "intriguing," but "eye-opening," the teacher candidate felt that including the subject, rather than explaining it, was enough:

> When I started, I was completely skeptical about the subject. But, as time went on, I was more and more intrigued by the subject. At first, I struggled with the topic because I wanted to touch the subject, but I did not want to dive in too deep. This is a topic that can be very touchy, and it was hard for me to grasp. But I really enjoyed the exposure I gained into the LGBTQIA+ community. This will be an issue I face in [my] everyday classroom in the future. I know where to find information and background stories.

While this teacher candidate evolved from feelings of fear to the actualization and realization of the essentialness of incorporating LGBTQIA+ content, curriculum, and rhetoric within their future classroom, this reflection demonstrates the defensive approach that defines this stage of the framework. Rather than seeking opportunities to incorporate and promote the recognition and inclusion of LGBTQIA+ students, their families, and allies, these teacher candidates state that they "know where to find information" when the time arises. This reactionary approach is antithetical to the full accomplishment of allyship because it recognizes diversity when it arises but does not actively promote it. Further, this teacher candidate never names LGBTQIA+ advocacy or allyship; instead, they continue to refer to the project as "the subject" or "the topic." This lack of specific and descriptive terminology also implies a generalization that is descriptive of empathy, but not allyship.

Another teacher candidate reflected they were "out of [their] element" when engaging with discussions about and creating materials for an LGBTQIA+ curriculum in the elementary classrooms. This candidate reflected that, despite the "very important" nature of the topic, they were preoccupied with the fear of causing "uproar" in their future classroom with parents and families of "the other kids." The reflection states:

> I do think and know this is a very important topic to teach all students. Students and teachers have to become more comfortable teaching and talking about these topics. LGBTQ [sic] children cannot thrive without the support they need. However, I am not equipped to answer questions students might ask me and so as of now, I would not want to go into the classroom and teach on this topic.

Again, despite a personal sense of empathy – as expressed in the language regarding the well-being of children, and the recognition of the necessity of discussing LGBTQIA+ topics in classrooms – this teacher candidate stops short of allyship because of the lack of actionable efforts or willingness toward true advocacy on a public platform (i.e., within classrooms). Reflections like these are not to be disregarded but emphasized for the missing component that will generate change within education settings: active engagement. The teacher candidate who appreciates but does not act upon the platitudes exemplified in these reflections is not yet combatting discrimination. This work has an appreciation that these candidates are not perpetuating harm or intolerance, nor are they acting prejudicially toward LGBTQIA+ students, families, and/or allies. But as we asked our students: is this enough? Especially in education?

During focus group discussions and interviews, teacher candidates were necessarily in a more public platform than experienced in the privacy of their own individual written reflection. When asked to discuss how research and engagement with LGBTQIA+ curriculum and pedagogical strategies had impacted their current views on incorporating such into their future classrooms. One candidate responded:

> My views stayed the same. I don't see it being a huge issue to promote in the classroom of elementary schools. Schools think children shouldn't . . . [long pause – 5+ seconds] okay I'm not saying this but . . . [pause] . . . it would be hard to introduce [issues related to the LGBTQIA+ community] at young ages. So I guess I'm saying I'm aware that issues could come up in my classroom and I know what to do and like what to tell them and how to answer questions but I would play it safe and not promote it. Like I don't think I would have the books [pertinent to LGBTQIA+ topics] in my classroom library.

Again, candidates are not dismissive of the importance of the topic. And, as evidenced by the indicated pauses and the deflection and justification of, "I'm not saying this but," the idea of dismissing issues pertinent to the LGBTQIA+ community is problematic for empathetic candidates. However, at this stage, there remains a missing engagement with promoting and intentional inclusion of LGBTQIA+ advocacy materials and rhetoric.

In fact, many of the empathic responsive data and artifacts seemed to respond to ideas and topics pertinent to LGBTQIA+ communities out of necessity, only. These responses are a departure for the second stage of the dimensions of allyship framework (e.g., passive engagement) because the response is intentional. Many of those data coded and resulting in the theme of "Passive Engagement" found that topics of LGBTQIA+ were addressed by accident or coincidentally as generalizations regarding diversity were referred. At the empathic responsiveness stage of the framework, topics pertinent to the LGBTQIA+ community, especially students and families, are addressed with intent, but that intent is explicitly defined by the compulsion to respond to students' questions. The idea of intentional incorporating and initiating discussions surrounding LGBTQIA+ advocacy and inclusion is still – to use the language of our teacher candidates – "uncomfortable," "touchy," and "difficult."

In several of the teacher candidates' multimodal books, as in many children's texts, animals represent people and populate the generated texts as the characters. As discussed in Burke and Copenhaver's (2004) consideration of children's literature, the use of animals in texts provides "intellectual and psychological distance" for the purpose of exploring those topics, powerful or painful, which we would not be comfortable exploring directly (Burke & Copenhaver, 2004, p. 207; Bishop, 2021). Many teacher candidates' multimodal books (greater than 50%) used this approach with animals depicting the main characters. As discussed previously, in one book, a cat and a dog debate the appropriateness of wearing their favorite color, despite stereotypes related to the colors pink and blue. In the below example, horses and unicorns accompany a story about the realities of differences celebration of being unique:

Figure 5.5 Horses Only – Example of Empathetic Responsiveness Text

While the celebration of diversity and the acknowledgment that individuality and expression are integral to identity is present, the use of anthropomorphism to discuss individuals constructs a limited gaze on the manifestation of individuality and does not teach young readers to recognize and celebrate differences in and among their peers. The use of anthropomorphic symbolism, as Burke and Copenhaver (2004) establish, does create the space for readers – even children – to become, "reflective and critical concerning life problems" (p. 212). However, the problem with these texts in the hands of those teachers – candidates who remain in the empathetic stage of the dimensions of allyship framework is that the step to initiate conversations is stunted and reactionary, rather than proactive. This presents the need to work toward actualizing the final stage of the framework – that of allyship and advocacy.

Allyship

Evidence of allyship is characterized in this work by discernable activism and engagement beyond stating personal opinions of support. Teacher candidate reflections that indicate allyship were not only receptive to acknowledging the importance of LGBTQIA+ inclusion in classroom curriculum and pedagogy but celebratory of the opportunity and necessity of such. Further, those candidates designated as demonstrating characteristics of the allyship stage of the framework expressed intentionality to initiate and advocate for the recognition, dismantling, and creation of viable alternatives to discrimination and systemic injustice. A characteristic of those data and artifacts coded as representing allyship was that many students were dismayed at the lack of their prior exposure. This was paired with a dedicated urgency to create resources and opportunities for exposure and inclusion pertinent to the LGBTQIA community now and in their future classrooms.

One teacher candidate expressed gratitude for the opportunity to engage in and with LGBTQIA+ curriculum materials and pertinent discussions because it was so notably absent in other coursework, and they felt unprepared for the realities of classroom teaching without such an opportunity:

> I am really grateful to have had the opportunity to learn more about the LGBTQIA+ community in a school setting. I knew I needed tools for my future classroom and I am glad to have research, books, and new ideas to add to my lesson plans. I especially will use reading and writing to allow children to learn about others without singling anyone out and express themselves to learn more about the world around them. I want to continue to learn ways to address and prevent bullying to create a safe and affirming learning environment for LGBTQIA+ students.

This teacher candidate has extended their engagement into allyship by actively promoting strategies – they mentioned reading and writing – to initiate discovery and conversations pertinent to LGBTQIA+ advocacy and inclusion, rather than just reacting to questions. Further, this reflection is emphatically a characteristic of the allyship stage of the framework when the teacher candidate addresses intentionality to create a learning environment that is both "safe" and "affirming" for LGBTQIA+ students, specifically. Many of the reflections in the other stages of the framework pushed for a generally "welcoming" environment and classroom for "all" students. While this is not prejudicial by itself, such generalizations do not centralize identities that depart from heteronormative points of view. The visibility actualized by this teacher candidate is a strong and wonderful exemplification of allyship.

Similarly, another teacher candidate reflected that researching, finding, and struggling to find curriculum dedicated to LGBTQIA+ advocacy and inclusion highlighted an alarming gap in their teacher education preparation and a weight on their shoulders that they feel obligated to carry into practice:

> I did not realize how much I did not know about the LGBTQIA+ community and how much I have not been prepared to bring up these subjects in my future classroom. I now believe it is necessary for me as a teacher to ensure that my students are informed and are more aware of the opportunities to include and be kind to members of the LGBTQIA [sic] community.

During one of the focus group discussions, another teacher candidate responded to the ways that exposure to LGBTQIA+ inclusive materials would impact their future class by saying,

> "I can actually be more inclusive [with these materials] now. I can actually create a more diverse environment and my kids can create a more diverse environment for themselves. I want to teach this stuff, not that they just learn it."

Both teacher candidates embody the difference between the stages of empathy and allyship in the framework because of the emphasis placed on the active and action-oriented mindset toward, not only welcoming LGBTQIA+ curriculum and pedagogy as part of an educational experience but, advocating for the necessity of creating opportunity and generating new spaces that are dedicated to LGBTQIA+ individuals, topics, and representation.

While those teacher candidates designated as in the empathetic stage of the framework acknowledged the importance of LGBTQIA+ inclusion when it arises, those data coded and resulting in the allyship stage of the framework progressed one step farther by intentionally pursuing inclusion. Not only is this distinct, but it is vital, especially within classrooms. As established, teacher candidates who resist the inclusion of LGBTQIA+ curriculum and pedagogy, even those without malintent, share that learning about such in elementary school feels "inappropriate" or "difficult" to discuss. However, classrooms – and elementary classrooms at that – are the nucleus of learning (Merrimack, 2020). They provide a dedicated setting and platform for students to ask questions, engage, and grasp concepts to understand the world in which they live (Annie E. Casey Foundation, 2010). Further, the average learning gain for students in kindergarten, first, and second grades is higher and more prolific than another other time during schooling (NCTE, 2018, 2021).

Given that elementary classrooms are the mainstay of children's learning (in American education), it is essential that LGBTQIA+ inclusion is situated as part of elementary curriculum and pedagogy in order to: (1) situate learning about LGBTQIA+ inclusion during these formative years of growth and development and (2) show young learners that learning about inclusion is just as necessary and normalized as learning about any number of other aptitudes. In reacting passively (i.e., "I will respond when my future students ask me questions" [about LGBTQIA+ students, families, and topics]), teacher candidates generate the rhetoric that their ability to ask questions is welcome in school, but the content of their question is not welcome.

As Steinberg (2011) advocates, it is essential that children learn as co-participants in studying and determining what is best for them (Steinberg, 2011, pp. 8–9). Further, children should remain intimately involved in shaping their social, psychological, and educational lives (Steinberg, 2011, p. 8). The allyship stage of the framework is defined by the creation of opportunities for LGBTQIA+ inclusion. As children are and should be essential to the constructs in the enactment of their learning, it maintains that allowing children to develop a "critical consciousness" of and about the world situates LGBTQIA+ inclusion firmly in classrooms, early, often, and most importantly, intentionally.

References

Annie E. Casey Foundation. (2010). Why reading by the end of third grade matters. *Kids Count Special Report*. https://www.aecf.org/resources/early-warning-why-reading-by-the-end-of-third-grade-matters

Bakhtin, M. M. (1981). The dialogic imagination: Four essays by M. M. Bakhtin (M. Holquist, Ed.; C. Emerson & M. Holquist, Trans.). Austin: University of Texas Press.

Bishop, R. S. (2021). A video interview with Rudine Sims Bishop. *Reading Rockets*. Retrieved from www.readingrockets.org/teaching/experts/rudine-sims-bishop

Bonilla-Silva, E. (2013). Rethinking whiteness studies. In *White out* (pp. 11–26). Lanham, MD: Rowman & Littlefield.

Brody, S. Gender-Inclusive Children's Literature as a Preventative Measure: Moving Beyond a Reactive Approach to LGBTQ+ Topics in the Classroom. *Facilitating Conversations on Difficult Topics in the Classroom: Teachers' Stories of Opening Spaces Using Children's Literature*, 60.

Burke, C. L., & Copenhaver, J. G. (2004). *Animals as people in literature*. Champaign, IL: National Council of Teachers of English.

Cassidy, J., & Kehler, M. (2018). "Holy gendered resource, batman!": Examining the broader application of comics and superhero fiction beyond their restrictive relationship with boys. In *Literacies, sexualities, and gender* (pp. 79–92). New York: Routledge.

Choi, J. A. (2008). Unlearning colorblind ideologies in education class. *Educational Foundations*, *22*, 53–71.

Joldersma, C. W. (2016). Doing justice today: A welcoming embrace for LGBT students in Christian schools. *International Journal of Christianity & Education*, *20*(1), 32–48.

Kendi, I. X. (2019). *How to be an antiracist*. New York: One World.

Marshall, E. (2004). Stripping for the wolf: Rethinking representations of gender in children's literature. *Reading Research Quarterly*, *39*(3), 256–270.

McEntarfer, H. K. (2016). *Navigating gender and sexuality in the classroom: Narrative insights from students and educators*. New York: Routledge.

Merrimack College (Ed.). (2020). Why is elementary education so important? *Elementary Education*. Retrieved from https://online.merrimack.edu/why-is-elementary-education-so-important/

NCTE. (2018). *Statement on gender and language*. Retrieved from https://tinyurl.com/NCTE-gender-and-language

NCTE. (2021). Guidelines for affirming gender diversity through ELA curriculum and pedagogy. *National Council of Teachers of English*. Retrieved from https://ncte.org/statement/guidelines-for-affirming-gender-diversity-through-ela-curriculum-and-pedagogy/

Pallotta-Chiarolli, M. (1999). Diary entries from the "teachers' professional development playground". *Journal of Homosexuality*, *36*(3–4), 183–205. https://doi.org/10.1300/J082v36n03_12

Payne, E., & Smith, M. (2011). The Reduction of Stigma in Schools: A New Professional Development Model for Empowering Educators to Support LGBTQ Students. *Journal of LGBTQ Youth*, *8*(2), 174–200.

Perez, M. J., & Salter, P. S. (2019). Trust, innocence, and individual responsibility: Neoliberal dreams of a colorblind peace. *Journal of Social Issues*, *75*(1), 267–285.

Robinson, K. H. (2013). *Innocence, knowledge and the construction of childhood: The contradictory nature of sexuality and censorship in children's contemporary lives*. New York: Routledge.

Robinson, K. H., & Davies, C. (2018). A history of constructions of child and youth sexualities: Innocence, vulnerability, and the construction of the normative citizen subject. In *Youth sexualities: Public feelings and contemporary cultural politics* [2 volumes], 1.

Steinberg, S. R. (2011). *Kinderculture: The corporate construction of childhood* (3rd ed.). Nashville, TN: Westview Press.

6 Challenges and Affordances

Preparing Elementary Teacher Candidates to Be Allies

We believe that the Dimensions of Allyship framework has promising implications for elementary teacher preparation and addresses a gap in the current literature. It provides a model for reflection and action on the part of faculty and candidates by creating space to move beyond LGBTQIA+ awareness to allyship. Although we do not see the framework as a means of assessing a particular stance, we do advocate for engaging elementary teacher candidates in discussions with LGBTQIA+ community members, in conducting research, and in creating multimodal texts as a meaningful point of entry into a more inclusive stance.

In addition, our data reflected those candidates felt more prepared to welcome LGBTQIA+ children and families into their future classrooms and believed themselves to be more knowledgeable and empathetic than they were at the start. However, with that said, their acceptance of all identities was not equal. Unfortunately, postsurvey data revealed that some students remained less accepting and felt less assuredness on their ability to act as allies for transgender children and/or parents even as they markedly increased in their acceptance of lesbian, gay, bisexual, queer, and intersex individuals. This remains an important area for future research and advocacy and is critical as teachers who are not welcoming and supportive of all youths, regardless of orientation and identity, may unwittingly contribute to what Wozolek, Wootton, and Demlow (2017) refer to as the school-to-coffin pipeline due to the suicides, suicidal ideation, and self-injurious behavior that have become an epidemic among LGBTQIA+ youth due in part to the discrimination faced in school settings (Suárez, Meister, & Lindner, 2019).

However, as we have illustrated, while some teacher candidates experienced shifts in their knowledge, understanding, and willingness to be allies for LGBTQIA+ students, others became more entrenched in their resistance and their participation was, at best, reluctantly given. We believe that this

DOI: 10.4324/9781003110934-6

strongly indicates the need for the inclusion of LGBTQIA+ topics in elementary teacher preparation programs. Although indeed, individual teacher candidates themselves may well be anti-homophobic and anti-transphobic, they are not given the tools, experiences, or resources to extend their personal beliefs into their professional identities and practice. As McEntefer (2016) argues:

> If gendered ways of being are formed in part in schools, and if heteronormativity and homophobia are experienced in different ways by boys and girls in schools, then the men and women who show up in teacher education classrooms as teacher candidates may have been differently shaped by the very discourse we are trying to prepare them to work against.
>
> (p. 56)

Broader and intentional implementation of allyship is required across education programs to promote action, rather than isolated reactions to specific events of discrimination. The passivity of bystanding, while social inequities continue, is just as harmful as the promotion of the social inequities themselves (Dryer, 2019). Thus, a more intentional approach in educator preparation is required that considers allyship an issue of human rights, rather than an isolated political maneuver. There is a gap in the development of preservice education that allows for the promotion of LGBTQIA+ equity only as a reaction to overt discrimination, rather than the intentional action of allyship (Hansen, 2015). Teacher preparation programs must be accountable for communicating relevant democratic, human rights perspectives to bridge the gap in preparation for dealing with the differing and complicated education contexts their candidates will encounter.

What is needed then is purposeful allyship in teacher education programs. Utilizing the stages described in the Dimensions of Allyship framework as potential guideposts for combatting ambivalence while encouraging steps toward advocacy, begins with being actively cognizant of the students we teach and an open willingness to learn more as teacher educators. Although we did not engage our colleagues as participants in this study, there is certainly a space for utilizing the framework to honestly interrogate our stances as teacher educators, as well as the position of our programs themselves. Indeed, as a potential avenue for future research, we believe it would be helpful for faculty to engage in professional development or study that mirrors some of what we asked our students to do. Establishing a culture that speaks out against injustice may change the overall atmosphere of a campus or program and positively impact the well-being of those in marginalized communities (Cornell Health, 2019). However, allyship is a practice that needs commitment, work, and focus, and often, efforts to create change or to disrupt the status quo are met with resistance (Kotter & Cohen, 2002).

Additionally, teacher candidates and teacher educators alike must be open to examining their own biases (Rife, 2019). Having a sense of self and own identity leads to the examination of one's beliefs and can ultimately help teachers, in-service and pre-service, disrupt notions based on differences (McGregor, Fleming, & Monk, 2015). However, this examination of one's own beliefs may also lead to a recognition of inadvertent complicity in discrimination toward individuals identifying as LGBTQIA+. As Mikulec and Miller (2017) remind us, preservice teachers have likely witnessed homophobic language, behaviors, or institutional practices that reify heteronormativity without knowing how, or if, to intervene. They may have even witnessed it in their programs, even as calls for diversity and inclusion increase. As we found in this study, preservice teachers often lack knowledge about the discrimination faced by LGBTQIA+ youth and thus also lack the language of advocacy and allyship, even if they might personally espouse notions of equitable and inclusive ideals.

There are multiple potential approaches to establishing a culture of allyship in education. Indeed, many teacher education programs often provide experiences that are designed to alter or shift one's belief system (McGregor, Fleming, & Monk, 2015). However, it is also true that most faculty and staff do not know how to address gender diversity and sexuality issues in the institutional context (Wickens & Sandlin, 2010). Neoliberal considerations that education is "objective" and approaches to diversity should utilize "even-handed relativistic neutrality" promote what Jones (2019) calls a "false equivalence" among diverse perspectives (p. 305). Moreover, as we have argued in previous chapters, issues involving gender expression/identity and sexual orientation do not enjoy the same level of inclusion as topics of diversity as do race, culture, religion, or language, which are now routinely included as "safe" topics (Pallotta-Chiarolli, 1999).

Yet, despite the moral panic that arises when the question of teaching about LGBTQIA+ identities and issues is raised, sexuality has always been present in schooling. As Foucault (1990) argued, however, sexuality is regulated in public discourse by that which is normalized and that which is pathological. In as much as heterosexuality is framed as "normal," and homosexuality, then as the opposite, is pathological. Heterosexuality is then the default unmarked and assumed boundary. Anything outside of that boundary poses a threat to the likewise unquestioned, unmarked boundary of "childhood innocence."

Challenging Heteronormative Constructions of Childhood

To examine and deconstruct these false dichotomies of normal and pathological sexualities and identities, teacher education and especially elementary teacher preparation, must also critically interrogate and reconstruct ideologies of "children" and "childhood" just as certainly as they do racism, sexism, and xenophobia (Wickens, 2016). This is needed because one of the most harmful barriers to the inclusion and recognition of LGBTQIA+ individuals and topics in elementary education is the trope of "childhood innocence" (Robinson, 2013). Long the rallying cry of far-right political and religious conservatives from the "Save Our Children" signs during the first wave of gay rights activism in the 1970s to the legislation initiatives currently being introduced in the United States, this social construction of the asexual child ironically in need of heteronormative protection forms the foundation for discrimination. This protection is often manifested in statements such as "children are too young to know about such things" which frames gender and sexual diversity as unknowable or even threatening topics that children should be protected from so that their innocence is maintained.

While some students lauded our "bravery" in structuring our classes around LGBTQIA+ topics, others found the controversial nature to be troubling and out of place in elementary education methods courses. This was exemplified in the final reflection of one student who wrote:

> I am out of my element. I found it really hard to write anything on this topic geared to this [elementary] age group. I think I found it so difficult because it wasn't and still is not often taught in schools. With many parents having different views on this topic I think it would cause a lot of uproar in my classroom and with families. All I could think about while doing this project is what type of questions the students are going to ask and am I ready and equipped to answer those questions.

The uproar from parents and other stakeholders, as well as the lack of preparedness she fears, is an indicative of the pervasive atmosphere of "moral panic" driven by conservative actors that dominates the landscape of elementary education (Robinson & Davies, 2018, p. 5). As Dyer (2017) discusses in her work on the social construction of the figure of the child as a site of both promise and peril for decentering heteronormativity, "the child is a dense site of meaning for both queer sociality and alienation. It is a locus of anxiety for homophobic culture because on it rests the reproduction of a heteronormative future" (p. 292). This position was certainly embedded and inscribed in the stance of many of our teacher candidates. The construction of the "child" as in need of heteronormative protection and practices was so natural as to be beyond question. While heterosexual social constructs and behavior are deemed appropriate for even the youngest child and reinforced in everything from the books on a classroom library shelf to the gendered roles apparent in imaginative play centers, the "dense site of meaning" is deeply rooted in heteronormativity and fear of even the slightest straying from its rigid contours. It is in this taken-for-granted stance that heterosexuality is a site of normalcy, of safety, and comfort, despite historical patriarchy, that we see an erasure of any threat or indeed "inappropriate" sexuality. As one of our students wrote in her reflection:

> Young children are being trained to associate colors, attitudes, occupations, and objects with gender. This is a major problem because the trainers do not know that they are training. In addition, it is also a problem because these stereotypes put restrictions on how people think.

She continued to address how early these stereotypes become ingrained and accepted by children by the third grade. Stereotypical binaries are firmly rooted and unquestioned:

> One of the levels I work with is a 4th grade class at Canyon Park Elementary School (pseudonym). These students have already decided their gender roles. I do not see any of the students questioning it. The same goes for the 3rd-grade classes that I observed at Lakeside Elementary School. However, the students that I teach and work with at the campus early childhood center are still moldable. By this, I mean that they do not conform to these stereotypes. These students do realize that certain things are more common. Nevertheless, these students understand that anyone can do anything they would like to do.

This "moldability" of the child speaks to the need for applying a queered lens to childhood, which acts as a remedy to traditional heteronormative, patriarchal constructions of the child (Dyer, 2017). Rather than framing the child as a blank slate on which to project hopes and fears of the future of heteronormative dominance, it allows for the multitude of possible identities children might construct for themselves. Far from being limited to only a sexual identity that may or may not include identifying as LGBTQIA+, a queered lens on childhood allows for and encourages identities that fall outside of binaries and "acceptable" social constructions of the child. This was exemplified in an example given by one of our students who worked in a preschool setting. One of her students, a little boy, loved to play dress-up in one of the centers in the classroom:

> I work at a daycare in the afternoons, and we have a dress-up box and a lot of the cool superheroes get taken and I have this one little boy who loves to put on the dresses and at first, his friends were like, "Come on, that's like a girl thing to do." Because when you are four, trucks are for guys, dancing is for girls and everything. So I just said, he likes the colors that look pretty. I would ask them if it does and they are like, "Yeah it does look pretty." Then we put it on him I would say, "Look how happy your friend is. He thinks he looks so handsome in this dress" and everything and just making them know those gender roles should not be a thing.

In this example, the teacher created a space for children to explore and engage in varying identities, which also allowed for a dialogue with other students about creating a space where differences are not merely tolerated but celebrated. The little boy's desire to put on a dress and the fact that it was acknowledged in a positive light as something that made him happy, allows for the other children to see a spectrum of identity and actions as normalized and worthy.

It is somewhat of a paradox then that when more typical or traditional approaches try to "protect" childhood innocence from the knowledge of various sexualities and gender variations, they also take away the opportunity for children to develop empathy and acceptance of those who may be different from themselves. It is also true that in avoiding discussions about LGBTQIA+ identities and experiences, teachers are teaching a lesson in silence and complicity in oppression. The silencing or absence of a gay "other" ensures that heteronormativity is affirmed, and any other way of being in the world is abnormal. However, young children, and certainly by the time they enter elementary school, have already heard words such as "gay," "lesbian," and "homosexual." Yet, it is almost a guarantee that they have heard those words uttered as a slur more often than not. For example, in our state, 94% of children and teens identifying as LGBTQIA+ report hearing the word "gay" as a slur regularly, 14% have heard it used derogatorily by school staff, and 31% report school staff making disparaging comments about students' gender expression. Moreover, 30% of LGBTQIA+ students, and 68% of transgender students, were unable to use the school bathroom aligned with their gender. Additionally, 22% of LGBTQIA+ students and 46% of transgender students were prevented from using their chosen names or pronouns in school (GLSEN, 2021).

This overt discrimination is rooted in schools being sites of heteronormativity and far from being asexual spaces, they overtly promote binary identities and the gendered roles that accompany them – as long as those roles and identities are heterosexual. This is underscored by the fact that in the same state, 26% of LGBTQIA+ students were disciplined for public displays of affection (PDA) that did not result in similar action for non-LGBTQIA+ students. Clearly, then schools accept the sexuality of their students if it conforms to the heterosexual norms that have functioned in schools as unquestioned boundaries. It is time to change the "schools as morality project" that has imposed rigid and vigilant regulation of sexuality and gender identity since public schooling began. We can think of no better place to start than with the pedagogy and curriculum of elementary teacher preparation.

Utilizing the Dimensions of Allyship Framework in Teacher Preparation

One of the key utilities of the Dimension of Allyship framework is that it presents us with a vehicle to think about how we might address resistance to allyship through dialogic exchange, self-reflection, and the creation of multimodal projects, such as children's books or designing infographics for school use. As preservice teacher candidates and faculty engage in these activities and where they themselves may be found in the stages of the framework, opportunities for critical reflection that allow for the examination of personal and professional identities become more readily available (McGregor et al., 2015; Rife, 2019). In thinking about those professional identities both teacher educators and preservice teachers might be able to identify and address gaps and silences in their practices and beliefs, as well as in the programs in which they participate.

However, this process may not be, and perhaps should not be, comfortable. As Kumashiro (2000) suggests, "Educators should expect their students to enter crisis. Since this crisis can lead toward liberating change, or toward more entrenched resistance, etc. . . . A space in the curriculum is needed for students to work through their crisis in a way that changes oppression" (p. 7). Many of our students did in fact enter a type of personal and/or professional crisis while examining their own beliefs and practices. During this exploration, we also engaged in an examination and reflection of what was constructed as normal and what was constructed as controversial. One of our students addressed this in her final reflection:

> I believe that this is a course that every student should have to take before getting into the classroom because as I said prior to this class, this topic was never discussed. This is very disappointing because this is a topic that needs to be discussed and not overlooked because of the controversy.

As well-intentioned and positive as this reflection was meant to be, the fact that the student frames LGBTQIA+ topics as "controversial" underscores Pallotta-Chiarolli (1999) point that the determination of "safe" and "unsafe" topics of diversity is still very much in play in both elementary and higher education. This student did not find discussions of race, culture, or religion to be controversial. Although discrimination and stereotypes around those areas of diversity are still unfortunately woven into our social landscape, they are not seen as too "controversial" to discuss in a teacher preparation course. However, the same does not hold true when gender and sexuality are included or intersect with the "safe" topics. Indeed, many of our students' reflections echoed the one shared earlier.

While there are complex and nuanced arguments for the comparison of racial discrimination and that based on gender and/or sexuality, it bears consideration. As Keenan (2012) argues, "current efforts to rebiologize sexual orientation might reflect or influence existing cultural anxieties and discourses about racialized bodies" (p. 167). Although we consider gender/sexuality discrimination as more of an intersection than a parallel to racism, some students began to independently make connections between racism and homo/transphobia. One student spoke of the integration and acceptance of LGBTQIA+ children as analogous to the racial integration of schools during the civil rights movement. Although we disagree with her premise that racial integration was "simple," during a focus group discussion, she noted the societal and generational norms that are challenged:

> It's as simple as the integration of schools. So you have white teachers learn how to deal with black children. So you had social norms that were being busted up and that's why you have to give us, and I think

> parents and teachers, and people in general, got to some way look at it like, you've got to allow them to kind of come up because it's breaking down norms in their head. That is a big deal to people, tradition, family, generational. That's a big deal. So I think that on one end, you have that make sure it's known, be comfortable with yourself, put it out there, put it in your truth.

The notion of having preservice elementary teachers put allyship "out there" as part of their truth is central to our argument for LGBTQIA+ inclusivity in elementary teacher education programs. As we have demonstrated earlier in this chapter and elsewhere, if teacher education is not prepared to be allies as part of our "truth," how can we possibly expect our candidates to demonstrate allyship or position themselves as change agents in the biased institution that is public education? How can they be prepared to challenge the moral panic exhibited by other stakeholders to provide spaces of equity and access for their LGBTQIA+ students and families? Throughout this study, we found that providing students with the opportunity to research topics related to LGBTQIA+ individuals, especially the issues faced by youth, built an empathy that was then reflected in their written work. Although we still encountered some resistance, the tacit and concrete activity of synthesizing what they learned into physical or digital text for their future elementary classrooms assisted them in strengthening their understanding of what it means to be an ally.

We believe that the curriculum and pedagogy in elementary teacher preparation courses could begin to incorporate critical dialogue surrounding intentional allyship more consciously. This then may lead to tangible products for curricular and pedagogical inclusion. For example, Pérez Echeverría and Scheuer (2009) describe how writing can shape knowledge and perceptions: "External representations [such as writing] are essential to construct knowledge, refine it, modify it, share and appropriate it" (p. 13). Certainly, low-stake opportunities such as multimodal writing or other content area projects can be facilitated in education methods courses to promote safe-space inclusion of members and allies of the LGBTQIA+ community, present texts that celebrate diverse family structures, and implement pedagogical choices that normalize a variety of identities and experiences. As we outlined in Chapter 3, there is great promise for integrating multimodal literacies, digital texts, and LGBTQIA+ inclusive children's literature to explore and create more equitable representation for LGBTQIA+ children and families.

One of the benefits of this approach is that it takes a familiar higher education structure – discussion, research, and class projects and branches it out to a topic that may be unfamiliar for many students. One student reflected,

> "during the research part of planning for the book, I was able to read many blog posts from students that were part of the LGBTQIA+ community. This was very informative and allowed me to learn even more about different individuals' situations."

This idea of attaching a topic that some students were ambivalent about to a familiar routine was echoed by several students. One spoke specifically about the dialogic space that was created where students could voice their opinions, their hesitancies, and fledgling strides toward allyship in a safe place:

> I felt that the classroom itself was a comfortable environment that allowed me to express my confusion, ask questions and hear personal stories. . . . I feel that I now understand more of the LGBTQIA+ community, I have become far more accepting and I have also gained a lot of new information.

Yet, for other students, the study and the book-making task led to some ambivalence and questioning of how to participate when the topic made them uncomfortable when approached as a K-5 teacher. This was evident in focus group discussions, where a student admitted,

> "I was very hesitant about the book we had to create. Not because I don't support the LGBTQIA+ community, but because how can I make them feel comfortable without [my] feeling uncomfortable?"

This equivocation was not uncommon and harkens back to Kumashiro's (2000) stance that crisis – even at this level of vacillation – can provide a space for students to grapple with challenging oppression is historically unjust systems such as public education. Thus, we were careful to maintain a space rooted in dialogic exchange and generative language to prevent the "entrenched resistance" Kumoshiro warned about (p. 7). For many students, however, they began to carry what they had learned forward into their pre-service experiences and/or early childhood positions they held on campus and elsewhere in the community.

One of the more heartening results of this study was the increase in the number of students who reported that they would be either "very prepared" or "moderately prepared" to address issues related to LGBTQIA+ students and families in their classrooms. Over the course of the two semesters, the percentage of students reporting that their self-assessed preparedness had improved after participation in the courses increased from just over 35% to almost 71% of the students surveyed in premeasures/postmeasures. Similarly, there was almost a 20% increase in the number of preservice teachers who indicated that they believed it would be appropriate to include discussions, lessons, or children's literature related to LGBTQIA+ issues/community in their classroom as part of the everyday curriculum. As we have shared previously, we are still cognizant of the work that remains to be done to engage students who did not experience a shift in belief and practice. However, for those who did experience a shift in beliefs as reported in the survey, also represented these changes in their written responses and discussions that were not anonymized as the survey had been. As one of our students stated:

> It's just simple things, like when you, write a short story, just have it be, "This girl and her girlfriend," or, "These two moms and their daughter," or just casually throwing it in there, so it's not a big deal, it's just something that they get used to seeing. So, when they do see it in their everyday life, they aren't shocked like, "That's different!" It's just one of those things that are thrown in there so casually, just like everything else. It's not a big deal. It becomes so typical.

Similarly, another preservice teacher who worked in the campus Child Development Center spoke of how easily she implemented what she learned in the study with her very young students:

> I was working [in the Center] the other day. They have a house area with a kitchen and stuff, toys, a castle, a ship, and everything. And one of the little boys said, "Can I go play by the house stuff?" And I was like, "Yeah, sure. Go ahead." And he was like, "Okay. I can?" And I was like, "Yeah, go for it." Even that little thing where. . . . I bet no one told him he can't, before, but he just didn't think he could. It's little things like that, just to normalize it, so there's not that question anymore.

These students' approaches to typifying LGBTQIA+ identities align with Lowenthal, Humphrey, Conley, et al. (2020) assertion that promoting inclusive classrooms should utilize assignments and approaches that promote previously unheard voices' and challenge assumptions. In this regard, queering elementary education preparation (Suárez et al., 2019) might also intersect with critical literacy practices such as questioning oppressive ideologies, while seeking the silenced voice drawing from local contexts, issues, and practices (Vasquez, Janks, & Comber, 2019).

This reflects not merely a pedagogical method, but rather a way of being in the world, or as Freire wrote, reading both the word and the world (Freire, 1993) to deconstruct heteronormativity and cisgender privilege.

Similarly, introducing the practice of reading queerly (Kumashiro, 2000) also allows for the queering of texts already staples in classroom libraries, by exploring the issues of power, identity, and justice from a different perspective and in a way that listens for voices missing or silenced in the dominant discourse of elementary education. Ryan and Hermann-Wilmart (2018) advocate for foundational literacy practices typical of elementary classrooms, to be grounded in queered readings of commonly found children's literature to explore the issues of discrimination when books with LGBTQIA+ characters are not present. Much like our student who disrupted the status quo in the early childhood setting by challenging traditional gender roles in the make-believe play center, so might teachers utilize the taken-for-granted assumptions evident in traditional children's literature to reflect allyship. Ideally, however, teacher education programs would utilize children and young adult literature with LGBTQIA+ characters in their methods courses to normalize the practice and to provide teacher candidates with both pedagogical and justice-based approaches. Just as critical, however, is the need to prepare future teachers to anticipate potential conservative stakeholder backlash when using books that feature LGBTQIA+ characters and have their counter-tactics and rationales constructed ahead of time. If we are to prepare our elementary teacher candidates to be allies for LGBTQIA+ children, we must rethink our curriculum. We too must model not just the strategies for content knowledge in our methods classes and across the entirety of our teacher education, including field placements. We must also teach them change agency (Shor, 2021) that is, how to engage in change-making within historically hegemonic societal structures. We must also model how to be advocates for children and/or parents who identify as LGBTQIA+. Anything short of that makes us complicit in oppression.

Future Directions for Research and Practice

Although we are proud of our teacher candidates for being open to participating in this study and for the movement toward allyship that many displayed, we are hesitant to call this project a success. The foremost reason for that is that the approaches and practices outlined here did not become an embedded component of our teacher education program. While we have been successful in adding an undergraduate critical sociocultural theories class to the core courses all must take, LGBTQIA+ representation in methods courses remains, at best, idiosyncratic to the course instructor. This then is certainly a limitation to this research, and other studies like it. Once the project comes to an end – especially those dependent of external funding – so does some of the momentum and hope for sustained change. We are hopeful that we will be able to continue to work with like-minded colleagues and administration in creating "critical friends" who will join us in efforts to promote pedagogical practice with an eye toward change (Blake & Gibson, 2021).

One of the ways this might be implemented using the Dimensions of Allyship as a model is to have discussions and faculty professional development to examine and acknowledge any ambivalence or bias we, as teacher educators may hold toward creating an LGBTQIA+ inclusive teacher preparation program and environment. It may be time to hold the mirror up and reflect on which dimensional stage in the framework we occupy. Recalling that over 60% of our participants did not feel that we had adequately prepared them for welcoming, much less advocating for the LGBTQIA+ students they will certainly have in their future classrooms, self and programmatic examination is a much needed first step.

Yet, we cannot stop with self-reflection and promises for inclusivity. As Gorski, Davis, and Reiter (2013) remind us, despite awareness of the need for inclusive practices, "silence persists in teacher education programs when it comes to LGBTQ concerns" (p. 227). We know too, then that a culture of silence leads to teacher candidates not being equipped with the knowledge and strategies necessary to be allies and advocates in their classrooms. We would rather see this research and others like it inform substantive change in the way college of education prepare their elementary students. We call for teacher candidates to do field placements in LGBTQIA centers or to volunteer in the same. We also see the need for partnerships with LGBTQIA+ community advocates to come work with our candidates. One of the experiences many of our preservice teachers mentioned as very beneficial was the opportunity to ask questions in a respectful but open manner with a member of the community.

With this said, however, the burden of educating straight and/or cisgender preservice teachers cannot be passed to or lie with the LGBTQIA+ community. It must be a collaborative effort of shared vision and our responsibility. To the extent that the Dimensions of Allyship framework might hold up a mirror for reflection followed by actionable steps, we look forward to furthering this line of research and following our candidates into their classrooms to examine what, if any, impact it has had on their beliefs, practices, and advocacy.

As we complete this book, we are both skeptical and optimistic about LGBTQIA+ inclusion in elementary teacher preparation. We are skeptical because as mentioned in the Introduction section, there are over 100 bills in state legislatures aiming to exclude transgender children from full education participation or to actively harm them by denying adequate medical care. We are skeptical too because of efforts in almost a dozen states to ban Critical Race Theory (Crenshaw, Gotanda, Peller, & Thomas, 1995) and/or to muzzle teachers when they attempt to teach a history of the United States that honestly reflects a past mired in systemic oppression alongside more admirable moments of liberation. On the other hand, we are optimistic that within their first 100 days in office, President Joe Biden and Vice President Kamala Harris rescinded the harmful cuts to LGBTQIA+ healthcare and anti-discrimination law of the previous administration. We are solemnly optimistic, that the Pulse nightclub in Orlando Florida, the site of the deadliest attack on LGBTQIA+ people in the United States, will be dedicated as a National Memorial. The memory of those lost there will not be silenced and instead will be "commemorated as hallowed ground" according to President Biden. Finally, we are optimistic because we were able to facilitate over 100 preservice teacher candidates to at the very least awareness and hopefully to allyship and advocacy for LGBTQIA+ children and families. While we cannot know for certain, we hope that the ripple effect of our experiences together has had a positive impact on their classrooms and the children who inhabit them.

References

Blake, J., & Gibson, A. (2021). Critical friends group protocols deepen conversations in collaborative action research projects. *Educational Action Research, 29*(1), 133–148.

Cornell Health (2019). Ally up! Practice Effective Allyship. *Cornell Health.* Retrieved from https://health.cornell.edu/sites/health/files/pdf-library/ally-up.pdf

Crenshaw, K., Gotanda, N., Peller, G., & Thomas, K. (1995). *Critical race theory. The key writings that formed the movement* (pp. 276–291). New York: The New Press.

Dryer, H. (2019). *The Queer Aesthetics of Childhood: Asymmetries of Innocence and the Cultural Politics of Child Development.* Rutgers University Press.

Dyer, H. (2017). Queer futurity and childhood innocence: Beyond the injury of development. *Global Studies of Childhood, 7*(3), 290–302.

Foucault, M. (1990). *The history of sexuality: An introduction, volume I.* Trans. Robert Hurley. New York: Vintage, 95.

Freire, P. (1993). *Pedagogy of the oppressed: New revised.* New York: Continuum.

GLSEN. (2021). *School climate for LGBTQ students in Virginia (state snapshot)*. New York: GLSEN.

Gorski, P. C., Davis, S. N., & Reiter, A. (2013). An examination of the (in)visibility of sexual orientation, heterosexism, homophobia, and other LGBTQ concerns in US multicultural teacher education coursework. *Journal of LGBT Youth, 10*(3), 224–248.

Hansen, L. E. (2015). Encouraging pre-service teachers to address issues of sexual orientation in their classrooms: Walking the walk & talking the talk. *Multicultural Education, 22*(2), 51–55.

Jones, T. (2019). A global human rights approach to pre-service teacher education on LGBTIs, *Asia-Pacific Journal of Teacher Education, 47*(3), 286–308, DOI: 10.1080/1359866X.2018.1555793

Keenan, D. (2012). Marriage and the Homosexual Body: It's About Race. *Journal of homosexuality, 59*(9), 1230–1258.

Kotter, J. P., & Cohen, D. S. (2002). *The Heart of Change Real-Life Stories of How People Change Their Organizations*. Harvard Business Press, Harvard.

Kumashiro, K. (2000). Teaching and learning through desire, crisis, and difference: Perverted reflections on anti-oppressive education. *The Radical Teacher*, (*58*), 6–11.

Lowenthal, P. R., Humphrey, M., Conley, Q., Dunlap, J. C., Greear, K., Lowenthal, A., & Giacumo, L. A. (2020). Creating Accessible and Inclusive Online Learning: Moving Beyond Compliance and Broadening the Discussion. *Quarterly Review of Distance Education, 21*(2), 1–82.

McEntarfer, H. K. (2016). *Navigating gender and sexuality in the classroom: Narrative insights from students and educators*. New York: Routledge.

McGregor, C., Fleming, A., & Monk, D. (2015). Social justice issues in initial teacher education in Canada: Issues and challenges. In Falkenberg, T.(Ed.). *Handbook of Canadian research in initial teacher education*. Ottawa, ON: Canadian Association for Teacher Education. ISBN 978-0-9947451-3-2. Retrievable from http://www. csse-scee. ca/associations/about/cate-acfe

Mikulec, E. A., & Miller, P. C. (Eds.). (2017). *Queering classrooms: Personal narratives and educational practice to support LGBTQ youth in schools*. Charlotte, NC: IAP.

Pallotta-Chiarolli, M. (1999). Diary entries from the "teachers' professional development playground". *Journal of Homosexuality, 36*(3–4), 183–205. https://doi.org/10.1300/J082v36n03_12

Perez Echeverria, M. P., & Scheuer, N. (2009). *Representational systems and practices as learning tools*. Rotterdam: Sense Publishing.

Rife, A. (2019). Missing the signs: Imperfect allyship and the re-examiniation of personal biases. *Kansas English, 100*(1), 23–26.

Robinson, K. H. (2013). *Innocence, knowledge and the construction of childhood: The contradictory nature of sexuality and censorship in children's contemporary lives*. New York: Routledge.

Robinson, K. H., & Davies, C. (2018). A history of constructions of child and youth sexualities : innocence, vulnerability, and the construction of the normative citizen subject. In S. Talburt (Ed.), *Youth Sexualities: Public Feelings and Contemporary*

Cultural Politics. Volume 1 (pp. 3–29). Retrieved from https://ebookcentral.proquest.com/lib/uwsau/reader.action?ppg=38&docID=5401003&tm=1542154650104

Ryan, C. L., & Hermann-Wilmarth, J. M. (2018). *Reading the rainbow: LGBTQ-inclusive literacy instruction in the elementary classroom.* Teachers College Press.

Shor, I. (2021). Personal correspondence.

Suárez, M. I., Meister, S. M., & Lindner, A. L. (2019). Envisioning queer curricula: A systematic review of LGBTIQ+ topics in teacher practitioner literature. *Journal of LGBT Youth*, 1–17.

Vasquez, V. M., Janks, H., & Comber, B. (2019). Critical literacy as a way of being and doing. *Language Arts, 96*(5), 300–311.

Wickens, C. M. (2016). Constructions of children and childhood. *Queering Classrooms: Personal Narratives and Educational Practices to Support LGBTQ Youth in Schools*, 45.

Wickens, C. M., & Sandlin, J. A. (2010). Homophobia and heterosexism in a college of education: A culture of fear, a culture of silence. *International Journal of Qualitative Studies in Education, 23*(6), 651–670.

Wozolek, B., Wootton, L., & Demlow, A. (2017). The school-to-coffin pipeline: Queer youth, suicide, and living the in-between. *Cultural Studies, Critical Methodologies, 17*(5), 392–398. https://doi.org/10.1177/1532708616673659

Index

Note: Page numbers in *italics* indicate a figure and page numbers in **bold** indicate a table on the corresponding page.

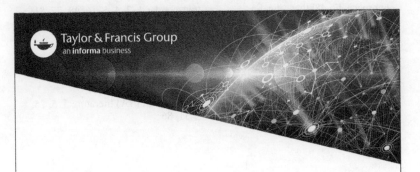

For Product Safety Concerns and Information please contact our EU
representative GPSR@taylorandfrancis.com Taylor & Francis Verlag GmbH,
Kaufingerstraße 24, 80331 München, Germany

Printed and bound by CPI Group (UK) Ltd, Croydon, CR0 4YY
08/06/2025
01896986-0004